D0579967

# THE HOLY SPIRIT, YOUR FINANCIAL ADVISOR

## Books by Dr. Creflo Dollar

*In the Presence of God*

*Live Without Fear*

*Not Guilty*

*Love, Live, and Enjoy Life*

*Breaking Out of Trouble*

*Walking in the Confidence of God in Troubled Times*

*Claim Your Victory Today*

*Winning in Troubled Times*

# THE HOLY SPIRIT, YOUR FINANCIAL ADVISOR

## God's Plan for Debt-Free Money Management

# DR. CREFLO DOLLAR

**Faith Words**

NEW YORK   BOSTON   NASHVILLE

This publication is designed to provide competent and reliable information regarding the subject matter covered. However, it is sold with the understanding that the author and publisher are not engaged in rendering legal, financial, or other professional advice. Laws and practices often vary from state to state and if legal or other expert assistance is required, the services of a professional should be sought. The author and publisher specifically disclaim any liability that is incurred from the use or application of the contents of this book.

Copyright © 2013 by Dr. Creflo Dollar
All rights reserved. In accordance with the U.S. Copyright Act of 1976, the scanning, uploading, and electronic sharing of any part of this book without the permission of the publisher is unlawful piracy and theft of the author's intellectual property. If you would like to use material from the book (other than for review purposes), prior written permission must be obtained by contacting the publisher at permissions@hbgusa.com. Thank you for your support of the author's rights.

Unless otherwise indicated, all Scripture quotations are taken from THE AMPLIFED BIBLE (AMP). THE AMPLIFIED BIBLE, OLD TESTAMENT, copyright © 1965, 1987 by The Zondervan Corporation. THE AMPLIFIED BIBLE NEW TESTAMENT, copyright © 1954, 1958, 1987 by The Lockman Foundation. Used by permission.

Scripture quotations marked (NLT) are taken from the Holy Bible, New Living Translation, copyright © 1996, 2004, 2007 by Tyndale House Foundation. Used by permission of Tyndale House Publishers, Inc., Carol Stream, Illinois 60188. All rights reserved.

Scripture taken from The Message (MSG). Copyright © 1993, 1994, 1995, 1996, 2000, 2001, 2002. Used by permission of NavPress Publishing Group.

Scripture quotations noted KJV are from the King James Version of the Holy Bible.

FaithWords
Hachette Book Group
237 Park Avenue
New York, NY 10017

faithwords.com

Printed in the United States of America

RRD-C

First Edition: September 2013
10 9 8 7 6 5 4 3 2 1

FaithWords is a division of Hachette Book Group, Inc.
The FaithWords name and logo are trademarks of Hachette Book Group, Inc.

The Hachette Speakers Bureau provides a wide range of authors for speaking events. To find out more, go to www.hachettespeakersbureau.com or call (866) 376-6591.

The publisher is not responsible for websites (or their content) that are not owned by the publisher.

ISBN 978-1-4555-7728-6

Library of Congress Control Number 2013939288

# CONTENTS

# INTRODUCTION

*Who Is the Holy Spirit?*

I have still many things to say to you, but you are
not able to bear them *or* to take them upon you
*or* to grasp them now. But when He, the Spirit
of Truth (the Truth-giving Spirit) comes, He
will guide you into all the Truth (the whole, full
Truth). For He will not speak His own message
[on His own authority]; but He will tell whatever
He hears [from the Father; He will give the
message that has been given to Him], and He will
announce *and* declare to you the things that are to
come [that will happen in the future].

—JOHN 16:12–13

The news media has tried repeatedly to cast a negative light on my ministry because I teach people that God wants them to prosper. As a result, some people think my success in ministry has come from some type of gimmick or wrongdoing. Some preachers have called me one of the "name-it-and-claim-it preachers." Those who speak negatively about me have chosen to believe that I had to do something wrong in order to achieve the success of World Changers Church International and Creflo Dollar Ministries.

However, the truth is, I can't give myself the credit for my success—all the credit belongs to God. I simply follow the leadership of the Holy Spirit in all that I do. The Holy Spirit has always led me to success, not just financially but in every arena of life. Words cannot express how much I appreciate having Him as my guide. Sometimes I become so overwhelmed with gratefulness that I have to stop at the side of the road and, right there in my car, give Him praise and thanksgiving. He deserves all the credit for every successful endeavor in my life.

For instance, He helped rescue me from death's grip in a horrible car accident in 2000; He helped our church purchase a $17 million World Dome debt free; He led me to my beautiful wife, Taffi, my spiritual father, Kenneth Copeland, and other great men and women in the body of Christ, and so much more! And God is not through with me yet! This is only the beginning!

I believe I am well qualified to teach on the subject of the Holy Spirit. I have not always followed His leading perfectly, but He has always gotten me to where I needed to be each time I have yielded to Him. The things He has led me to do don't always make sense to other people, but His leading always agrees with God's will. He has always led me to truth, and He continues to give me new revelations as I continue to grow in ministry.

Some people think the Holy Spirit is spooky or a feeling. If you are one of those people, allow me to introduce you to Him. You will find that there is nothing spooky about the Holy Spirit. As a matter of fact, I don't see how a Christian can be effective in life without Him. I call Him my unseen partner, and if you are a born-again Christian, He is also *your* unseen partner. The day you accepted Jesus as your Lord and Savior, the Holy Spirit came to dwell inside your re-created spirit. Yes, He's in there! And He wants you to acknowledge His presence (John 14:16–17).

The subject of the Holy Spirit is one of the most misunderstood and misinterpreted subjects among Christians and non-Christians. Many people are afraid to hear sermons about the Holy Spirit because of incorrect teachings and doctrines. The topic of speaking in tongues and the gifts of the Spirit are often shunned with fear. However, there is nothing fearful about Him. He doesn't seek to harm us but to comfort and guide us. He desires to work through us so that we can experience the power that God ordained every Christian to have and use in these last days.

---

*The subject of the Holy Spirit is one of the most misunderstood and misinterpreted subjects among Christians and non-Christians.*

---

Gaining an understanding of who the Holy Spirit is, and who He isn't, is critical to experiencing His presence and power. The Holy Spirit is *not* a feeling or an emotion. Although His presence can stir up holy emotions within you, He is actually the third person of the Trinity—God the Father, God the Son, and God the Holy Spirit. As I mentioned earlier, your re-created spirit is His dwelling place. As you learn to yield to Him, you will find yourself working out God's plan for your life. In addition, you will experience supernatural power and breakthrough like never before.

Jesus explains the function of the Holy Spirit in John 16:7, *"Nevertheless I tell you the truth: It is expedient for you that I go away: for if I go not away, the Comforter will not come unto you; but if I depart, I will send him unto you."* Jesus knew He would have to leave in order for the Holy Spirit to come to the earth. Now that the Holy Spirit is here, and dwelling in every born-again Believer, the power of God can flow to an even greater extent than when Jesus walked the earth!

The Holy Spirit is the motivator, energizer, and operator of every revealed plan or vision from God. He is the Spirit of Truth and has been sent to reveal the mind of God to Believers (John 16:12–13). He has come to reveal wisdom, knowledge, abilities, and mysteries to us to show us our significance, value, and power. He is also the revealer of the hidden treasures of the kingdom of God and holds the key to the inheritance of the saints. He wants to reveal our God-nature to us and cause us to live on a higher level than we are living right now. He is the most valuable asset to Christian living, and yet many times Believers don't know enough about Him to really take advantage of what He can do in their lives.

*The Holy Spirit is the motivator, energizer, and operator of every revealed plan or vision from God.*

Since we are living in the last days, it is imperative that we know how to distinguish the Holy Spirit's voice. The hunches (or inner nudges) we receive that either direct us or warn us are the promptings from the Holy Spirit. We can develop a discernment of His voice through the study and meditation of the Word of God. He will never say anything to us that doesn't line up with the written Word, so studying the Bible is essential to recognizing His voice. Praying in tongues also helps to sharpen our spiritual discernment and awareness of Him. It may take some time to become proficient in recognizing His voice, but as you develop, pay attention to whether or not you have peace in your spirit about something you are about to do. If you don't have peace, most likely the Holy Spirit is warning you not to proceed.

When you acknowledge the Holy Spirit and commune with Him on a daily basis, He will show you mysteries and the secret plans of God for your life. Jeremiah 33:3 says, *"Call unto me, and I will answer thee, and show thee great and mighty things, which thou knowest not"* (KJV). He will guide you into your destiny when you allow Him to direct your decisions.

You can cultivate your relationship with the Holy Spirit by praising God, praying, and singing spiritual songs (Ephesians 5:19). Doing these things helps you become more sensitive to His presence. He wants to be acknowledged, and He wants to talk to you. When you call on the Holy Spirit, you may say, "Holy Spirit, I don't know what to do in this situation, but I know you know the answer. Show me what to do." Spend some time praying in the Spirit and then wait on Him until you hear Him speak to you. When you call, He will answer.

Since the Holy Spirit was sent to help guide and direct your life, it is important that you set aside time every day to fellowship with Him. Talk with Him as you would a close friend or family member. Talk to Him about your concerns and about the Scriptures. He will give you the revelation, insight, and enlightenment you need to fulfill God's plan for your life.

Developing a relationship with the Holy Spirit is like developing a relationship with a close friend. He is just as real as the friends you can see. Like all relationships, your relationship with the Holy Spirit will require quality time. You may need to get up earlier in the morning to pray. When you begin to have a relationship with the Holy Spirit, the rewards far outweigh any inconveniences.

---

*Developing a relationship with the Holy Spirit is like developing a relationship with a close friend.*

---

## The Holy Spirit and Your Finances

Most of us are cautious about any advice we receive concerning our finances. We like to feel we are in total control where our finances are concerned. However, when we allow the Holy Spirit to speak to us about our finances, He will lead us to real profit. He will help us avoid the financial pitfalls that plague most people living according to the dictates of society. The Holy Spirit gives us supernatural wisdom to manage our money wisely on a day-to-day basis.

In order to hear His directions, we must change our thinking and make sure it agrees with the Word of God. When the Holy Spirit speaks, He agrees with the Word of God. He gives us peace in our spirits, which is how we recognize His voice from all the other voices we hear within.

## How to Use This Book

As someone who has received many questions about finances, I felt it was time to write a book that addresses the financial issues people face on a daily basis. As a pastor, I want people to understand that God has a plan for their finances. The Holy Spirit is a very present help in our time of need. He helps us whenever we need guidance. The one thing we have to learn to do is yield to Him. I understand that being led by the Holy Spirit is not always as easy as it sounds. However, when we follow His leading, He will lead us to great success.

This book is not to be read for entertainment. It should be used as a tool to help you yield to the Holy Spirit when it comes to making wise financial decisions. At the end of each chapter, there are discussion questions that will allow you to write whatever the Holy Spirit places on your heart. This may be the most powerful journey you will ever take! So grab a pen and, if needed, a journal for extra writing space, and get ready to be changed forever!

# THE HOLY SPIRIT, YOUR FINANCIAL ADVISOR

# KNOWLEDGE OF HIS WORD
# PREPARES OUR HEARING

1

O taste and see that the Lord [our God] is good!
Blessed (happy, fortunate, to be envied) is the
man who trusts and takes refuge in Him.

—PSALM 34:8

Every Scripture is God-breathed (given by His
inspiration) and profitable for instruction, for
reproof *and* conviction of sin, for correction
of error *and* discipline in obedience, [and] for
training in righteousness (in holy living, in
conformity to God's will in thought, purpose,
and action)...

—2 TIMOTHY 3:16

[And I pray] that the participation in and sharing
of your faith may produce and promote full
recognition and appreciation and understanding
and precise knowledge of every good [thing] that
is ours in [our identification with] Christ Jesus
[and unto His glory].

—PHILEMON 1:6

Several years ago, I experienced a very interesting situation. I was dealing with a business contractor and became very frustrated because I thought a particular product was going to be turned over to me, but it did not work out that way. Since the product was already paid for, I became extremely frustrated. My sleep was disturbed because I was so agitated, and I spent the night trying to figure out how to legally resolve the situation. Not once did I acknowledge the true solution—God and His Word.

The next morning I woke up feeling the same frustration. I began to pray in the Spirit, and God interrupted me. He said, "Why are you allowing this situation to steal your peace and frustrate you?" I told the Lord all about how I thought it wasn't fair and so forth. He said, "I want to teach you something about trust."

He began dealing with me about trusting Him. Proverbs 3:5 says, *"Lean on, trust in, and be confident in the Lord with all your heart and mind and do not rely on your own insight or understanding."* I was leaning on my own insight and understanding. Once I placed my trust and confidence in God's ability to handle the situation, I was no longer frustrated, and I received the solution I needed.

I have discovered that some of the greatest manifestations in the Bible came as a result of reliance and confidence in God. I have also discovered that many times people *believe* God, but they don't *trust* Him. Actually, I believe they sometimes confuse the two. When we trust God, we rely and depend on Him to work out the situation.

---

*I have also discovered that many times people* **believe** *God, but they don't* **trust** *Him.*

---

It is not unusual for people to confuse faith and trust. However, there is a difference between the two. Faith is a practical expression of the confidence we have in God and His Word, while trust is a practical expression of our commitment to God and His Word. The question is, how committed do we remain to God and His Word when it comes to issues in life that irritate us? A sure indication of a lack of trust is frustration. In other words, whenever a situation robs us of our peace, we are not trusting God.

When it comes to our finances, we are often faced with challenges. But we can maintain our peace by trusting God to meet our needs. We must say, and mean, "Everything is going to be just fine." That is what trust is all about. It is a lifetime commitment to rely on God no matter what challenges we face in life. Many times, I have had to say, "Well, God, I don't know how you are going to do this, or when, but I trust you." Because I have developed my trust in God, I am no longer disturbed by irritating circumstances. Whenever they arise, I simply look to Him and say, "Lord, I trust you, and I know that everything will be just fine."

## Trusting Him and His Word

God revealed to me that trusting Him is similar to following directions in order to reach a certain destination. When you need to get somewhere you've never been before, and someone who already knows the way gives you directions, you don't question that person. You simply follow the directions you are given. In other words, you trust that he or she knows how to get you to your destination. Even if you get lost, perhaps because you misunderstood something or missed a turn, you could even call that person to clarify the directions and then get back on the right road. Similarly, you must call on God for directions in life. He has given us directions—His written Word—to the destination He has chosen for us. When you miss it or make a mistake, God will direct you through His written Word and make sure you get back on the right path.

In order to develop complete trust in our Heavenly Father, we must cultivate our relationship with Him every day. Just as we develop our trust in others by spending time with them, we likewise learn to trust God the same way. We spend time with Him by meditating on the Word (repeating Scriptures over and over in our minds until revelation knowledge comes) and reading the Word daily. In addition, spending time with God regularly in prayer is another way to develop a consciousness of His presence and voice, both of which help us develop trust in Him.

*In order to develop complete trust in our Heavenly Father, we must cultivate our relationship with Him every day.*

On the other hand, when we decide to trust our feelings, education, perceptions, or our own way of doing things, we basically say to God, "I don't trust *your* way." This is pride. However, when we choose to trust God and His Word as an act of our will, no matter what it may look like in the natural, we demonstrate humility through our trust in His directions. By making the Word our final authority and making a quality decision to place our faith in God at all costs, we experience His best in every situation.

## First Base Is the Word

I always tell people, "The Holy Spirit will save you time and money." Since He speaks in line with the Word, we must know what the Word says in order to recognize the Holy Spirit's voice. Therefore, if we want to receive revelation from God that will eliminate chaos in our lives, we cannot neglect His written Word. It is vital to have knowledge of God's Word. It will escort us into intimate places with God, and within those intimate places we will hear His voice giving us specific instructions.

Revelation (or wisdom) that comes from God is critical to our success when dealing with our finances. Revelation is the key to breakthrough and gives advantages that are not found in the world, because God's success is unlimited and immeasurable. We can't lose when we hear a rhema (specific, spoken) Word from the Lord. However, mere knowledge without revelation is limited. When He gives us revelation, He includes His instructions.

*Revelation is the key to breakthrough and gives advantages that are not found in the world.*

I thank God for the revelation I've received over the years in the area of finances. I totally rely on God where my finances are concerned. When He tells me to sow a seed, I do it. I'm quick to walk in obedience because I know that His way is the best way. So, to ensure that I remain in a position to hear from Him, I constantly renew my mind with the Word.

## The Word Instructs Us in the Basic Doctrines of God

Galatians 1:8 says, *"But even if we or an angel from heaven should preach to you a gospel contrary to and different from that which we preached to you, let him be accursed (anathema, devoted to destruction, doomed to eternal punishment)!"*

His Word instructs us in the basic doctrines or teachings of God. The more time we spend reading, studying, and meditating on God's Word, the more we develop the ability to distinguish between truth and error.

For instance, I counseled a Christian woman who insisted that the Lord told her to marry an unsaved man, which did not line up with the Word. However, God's Word tells us not to be unequally yoked with unbelievers (2 Corinthians 6:14). This woman had allowed the voice of the enemy to deceive her and lead her away from the truth and into error. The enemy is always seeking to take us in a direction that will destroy us.

*The enemy is always seeking to take us in a direction that will destroy us.*

When a Christian is deceived, I often wonder how much time that person has spent in the Word. Apparently he or she hasn't spent enough time in the Word to distinguish God's voice from the lying voice of Satan. However, we can prepare to hear God's voice by spending time reading and studying His Word. We can't be led by our desires; we must humble ourselves and find out what the Word says about our situation. If we don't, our selfishness will take over, allowing the enemy to take advantage of our lack of knowledge where the Word is concerned.

## The Word Helps Us Perceive Spiritual Reality

As human beings, we are comprised of three parts. We are spirit beings at the core; we have a soul, and we live in a physical body. First Thessalonians 5:23 states: *"And the very God of peace sanctify you wholly; and I pray God your whole spirit and soul and body be preserved blameless unto the coming of our Lord Jesus Christ"* (KJV).

The spirit is completely re-created at the point of salvation. We were made new creatures in Christ when we become born again. Second Corinthians 5:17 says, *"Therefore if any man be in Christ, he is a new creature: old things are passed away; behold, all things are become new"* (KJV). The transformation that took place within our spirits has to work its way into the soul and the body. For instance, when I became a born-again Christian, my spirit became new, but my mind and body stayed the same. It is my responsibility to make both my mind and body line up with my spirit.

*It is my responsibility to make both my mind*
*and body line up with my spirit.*

Andrew Wommack, in his online article "Spirit, Soul, and Body," wrote:

> In your soul, old things did not pass away, and all things haven't yet become new. For that reason, you could actually

*die from sickness or disease even though all of the power that raised Jesus from the dead is residing untapped within your spirit. It's like dying of thirst while leaning against a well full of life-giving water.*

*Think of your soul like the valve on a faucet: it controls the rate and volume of the flow of the spirit into your body. If your mind is renewed and in agreement with the Word, the valve is wide open. But if it is in agreement with what your body is feeling or what your emotions are experiencing, then the valve is closed to God's life in your spirit.*[1]

The soul is comprised of the mind, will, emotions, conscience, and imagination. When most people are referring to someone's personality, they are actually referring to the soul. The central control center of the soul is the mind. Therefore, the mind is the battlefield and will determine whether or not we have victory or defeat in our Christian lives.

This is why the Bible instructs us to renew our minds with God's Word. The Word keeps us in God's perfect will for our lives. Romans 12:2 says, *"Do not be conformed to this world (this age) [fashioned after and adapted to its external, superficial customs], but be transformed (changed) by the [entire] renewal of your mind [by its new ideals and its new attitude] so that you may prove [for yourselves] what is the good and acceptable and perfect will of God, even the thing which is good and acceptable and perfect [in His sight for you]."*

In order to tap into the resources we have within our spirits, mind renewal is imperative, as well as making a decision to believe the Word of God despite what is going on in the natural world. In James 1:23, the Word of God is compared to a mirror. When you look into a mirror, you can see your reflection. You trust that reflection so much that you rely on it to fix your hair and make other necessary adjustments to your appearance. You should trust the Word of God in the same manner. When you look into the mirror of the Word, you will see your true identity. It reveals your spiritual reality and shows you who you are at the core—within your spirit—so that you can make any necessary adjustments.

*In order to tap into the resources we have within our spirits, mind renewal is imperative.*

Our born-again spirits are the part of us that is like God. Our spirits believe the Word and agree with it. Also, the Holy Spirit dwells within us, and He speaks to our spirits. From our spirits flow the revealed knowledge of God. However, if our minds are not aligned with our spirits, we will dismiss the knowledge we receive and instead rely on our own thoughts.

Some Christians allow their sensual desires to lead and guide them instead of the Holy Spirit. They govern themselves primarily by their senses. Our senses are designed to help us interact in this physical world only. They should not be leading our lives. Instead, our lives should be governed by the Word. By being anchored in the Word, we won't be moved when our finances are attacked. The Word helps us remember that by God's grace our needs will be abundantly supplied. Additionally, 2 Corinthians 9:8 states: *"And God is able to make all grace (every favor and earthly blessing) come to you in abundance, so that you may always and under all circumstances and whatever the need be self-sufficient [possessing enough to require no aid or support and furnished in abundance for every good work and charitable donation]."* The Word is our seed, and it grows within us. As a result, when the attack comes, Satan is defeated quickly because we are established in the Word of God.

*By being anchored in the Word, we won't be moved
when our finances are attacked.*

## The Word Unlocks the Power Within

Within our spirits, we possess supernatural ability and might.
To transfer the power that lies within us to the natural realm, we
must begin to acknowledge the good that is within our spirits
(Philemon 1:4–6). The spirit of a person is completely re-created
at the point of salvation. Everything we will ever need for life and
eternity has already been placed within our spirits.

Ephesians 1:3 says, *"May blessing (praise, laudation, and eulogy) be
to the God and Father of our Lord Jesus Christ (the Messiah), Who has
blessed us in Christ with every spiritual (given by the Holy Spirit) blessing in the heavenly realm."* As a result, we become new creatures in
Christ (2 Corinthians 5:17–18).

The Apostle Paul describes the power that we have inside of us
in further detail in Ephesians 1:17–20:

> *[For I always pray to] the God of our Lord Jesus Christ, the
> Father of glory, that He may grant you a spirit of wisdom
> and revelation [of insight into mysteries and secrets] in the
> [deep and intimate] knowledge of Him, by having the eyes
> of your heart flooded with light, so that you can know and
> understand the hope to which He has called you, and how
> rich is His glorious inheritance in the saints [His set-apart
> ones]. And [so that you can know and understand] what is
> the immeasurable and unlimited and surpassing greatness of*

*His power in and for us who believe, as demonstrated in the working of His mighty strength, which He exerted in Christ when He raised Him from the dead and seated Him at His [own] right hand in the heavenly [places].*

If we do not *know* about spiritual reality, we won't know about the power we have within because we can't *feel* spiritual reality. The only way we can perceive and access what is in our spirits is through the study of the Word of God. The Word teaches us about what we have on the inside and how to unlock that power. It is only when our souls line up with our spirits (Romans 7:22) that we gain access to all the power and heavenly resources residing inside our spirits.

---

*The only way we can perceive and access what is in our spirits is through the study of the Word of God.*

---

## Practically Applying the Word

We don't have to lose sleep worrying about how we are going to get out of debt, pay our bills, or deal with other financial issues. We do not have to get upset when the world's economic system fails or when someone treats us unfairly, because we live according to another system—the kingdom of God system.

Now that we understand how to prepare ourselves to hear, we can begin the process of renewing our minds and receiving His instructions.

# Life Application

Begin to acknowledge the supernatural power you have within. Consistently cultivate this power by daily meditating on the Word concerning all the great, divine gifts you have. Here are some confessions to get you started:

### Declarations

- I have God's divine wisdom within me. I am filled with the knowledge of His will in all wisdom and spiritual understanding (Colossians 1:9).

- I possess supernatural wisdom and revelation, which enables me to receive the provision I need in every area of my life (Ephesians 1: 17 AMP).

- God has given me the wisdom to understand what to do to prosper in every way (3 John 2; Ephesians 1:17).

- I have been made a new creature in Christ (2 Corinthians 5:17 AMP). I understand that the transformation that took place within my spirit has to work its way into my soul and body. Therefore, I transform my mind by reading and studying the Word of God daily (Romans 12:2 AMP)!

- Everything I will ever need for this life and eternity is already within me (Ephesians 1:3; 2 Peter 1:3).

- I have might—which is the ability to do anything—residing inside of me now (Ephesians 3:16 AMP)!

- The power within me cannot be measured or limited. I have the fullness of God's power (Ephesians 1:18–19 AMP; John 1:16).

- I can transfer the power within my born-again spirit into the natural by acknowledging every good thing that is within me (Philemon 1:4–6).

- I am God's workmanship. He made me a new creation (Ephesians 2:10).

- I have received the abundance of grace and the gift of righteousness. I reign as a king in life through Jesus Christ (Romans 5:17).

# HEARING AND 2 OBEYING HIM

For this reason I am telling you, whatever you ask
for in prayer, believe (trust and be confident) that
it is granted to you, and you will [get it].

—MARK 11:24

But if you will indeed listen to and obey His
voice and all that I speak, then I will be an
enemy to your enemies and an adversary to your
adversaries.

—EXODUS 23:22

And after the earthquake a fire, but the Lord was
not in the fire; and after the fire [a sound of gentle
stillness and] a still, small voice.

—1 KINGS 19:12

Be unceasing in prayer [praying perseveringly]...

—1 THESSALONIANS 5:17

Many years ago when I first got saved, I was baptized by a prophet of God who had a vision of me preaching in a large, round building. At the time, I didn't really understand what his vision meant. Many years later, when our church began to grow to such a point where we needed a larger sanctuary, I knew I had to depend on the Holy Spirit's guidance to make it happen. It was then that God began to speak to me about this round building that was prophesied to me. As I began making plans for building, I learned it would cost $17 million, which our church didn't have at the time. However, God said we would build the church debt free!

God began giving me instructions on how to accomplish this great task, and we stepped out on faith. We hung architectural drawings and a model of the completed Dome in the chapel. Every Sunday, we stretched our hands toward those drawings and declared that the required finances to build the Dome were available and every need would be met. Our faith proved to be an unstoppable force. It wasn't long before I received revelation that we didn't need the entire $17 million to get started. We only needed to be obedient to God each step of the way.

*We only needed to be obedient to*
*God each step of the way.*

The first thing He told us to do was dig a hole. We had enough money to clear the land, so we had a ceremony and dug a hole. Soon after that, we laid the foundation and put up the columns. Before we knew it, the vision began to speak for itself, and we no longer needed the pictures. We could see the vision becoming a reality before our eyes. Three years after that first hole was dug, members of World Changers Church International moved into the World Dome, on December 24, 1995.

Hearing from God is a privilege that has been made available to us through the shed blood of Jesus. We no longer have to go through a variety of priests or be ceremonially cleansed before entering into communion with the Almighty. God desires that we position ourselves to hear His voice so we can receive the Word that will change our lives forever. Unfortunately, there are Christians who believe they cannot hear God's voice, which makes me wonder if they are really listening. God is a great conversationalist. And He will speak to us at any time, whether we're driving, sitting still, or standing in the presence of others. He'll tell us things that will bless our socks off, if we will only listen. *"And thine ears shall hear a word behind thee, saying, This is the way, walk ye in it, when ye turn to the right hand, and when ye turn to the left"* (Isaiah 30:21 KJV).

## Speaking His Language

Hearing God's voice requires that we have moments of silence for listening. Often when Christians pray, they do all the talking. However, a monologue is not a conversation. Our prayers should not be an endless talking session. If we talked endlessly in conversation with our friends, we would see their eyes glaze over as they grew weary of our endless chatter. The fact is, it's difficult to communicate with someone who talks so much that no one else can get a word in edgewise.

*Hearing God's voice requires that we have
moments of silence for listening.*

It is important to understand that contrary to common religious beliefs, prayer is *not* pleading with God or bargaining with Him to act on our behalf. Nor is it characterized by a lot of "spiritual" sounding clichés that do not line up with the Word. Prayer is simply communicating with God by speaking His Word to Him in faith. In other words, we must speak His language. When we pray this way, results are inevitable.

Hebrews 4:12 clearly describes the power of the Word. It says, "For the word of God is quick, and powerful, and sharper than any two-edged sword, piercing even to the dividing asunder of soul and spirit, and of the joints and marrow, and is a discerner of the thoughts and intents of the heart" (KJV). Verse 14 encourages believers to "hold fast to our profession." In other words, speak God's Word, because it is power-packed! When we pray, believing that we have already received what we are praying for, we will receive the answers to our prayers (Mark 11:24).

Prayer should produce rest, or peace of mind. Many people pray fear-based prayers and *hope* they are getting through to God, but they really don't have confidence in what they are praying. The Bible says that when we believe the Word, we will enter into a state of rest.

The integrity of the Word speaks for itself and will never fail. By allowing the Word to be the foundation of our prayer lives, our confidence in our prayers will soar to new heights. We must know in our "knower" that Scripture is infallible, have no doubt that what

God says is true, and believe that we already possess what we have prayed for. I urge you to begin to pray the solution to your problems *first*, rather than bombard heaven with empty, desperate pleas.

Prayer is the language through which you and the Father fellowship with each other. It is through your dialogue with Him that your faith in His promises through Jesus Christ will develop and grow. As you spend time with Him in prayer, you will begin to recognize His voice more clearly. He desires to direct you at every turn, and a developed prayer life will make it easier for Him to guide you.

Every failure in life is a prayer failure. God has already done everything He is going to do; the work has already been completed. Our job is to pray faith-filled prayers that are based on His Word and expect to receive results. Make no mistake about it; prayer is absolutely essential to our walking in the manifestation of God's promises. It is a key to getting results as a Christian.

---

*Prayer is absolutely essential to our walking in the manifestation of God's promises.*

---

Our prayers are heard. When we make the Word of God the foundation of our prayer life, we are guaranteed victory. We must not allow religion or tradition to blind us to the truth of what prayer really is. Our future depends on it.

## Tuning In to His Frequency

Reading the Word and spending personal time with God puts us on God's frequency so that we are able to recognize His voice. To understand this concept with more clarity, we can think of our favorite radio station. The station is always playing our favorite tunes throughout the day; however, we are not always tuned in. Although the signal remains constant, our involvement with the station depends on our decision to turn the radio on and tune in! Likewise, with God, He doesn't change His frequency or location. Like a radio station, He is always in operation, but we are not always tuned in to hear Him.

God is always speaking. However, if you are not hearing His voice the way you would like to, there may be something blocking your hearing. Here are some things that may be preventing you from hearing God's voice.

## 1. Unbelief

God operates by faith. If we are operating in doubt and unbelief, we are on a different frequency and will not be able to hear His voice. I've met people who were shocked to hear me say, "Here's what God told me this morning…" They looked at me as if I'd lost my mind! The truth is, God desires to share things with us just as He did with Abraham, Moses, David, Solomon, and other great men and women of God.

Paul warned us in Hebrews 3:12 not to have "an evil heart of unbelief" (KJV). By diligently studying the Word of God, we discover for ourselves what God has to say about the issues that concern us. It's impossible to have enough faith to believe in something unless you read the Word and find out what God has to say about it. The Bible is a book of promises from a loving Father to His children. If we can find it in there—whatever it may be—He wants us to have it. And that includes debt release and financial freedom! We must decide whether we will continue to walk in doubt and unbelief, or place our faith and trust that God will enable us to receive His best.

*The Bible is a book of promises from a loving*
*Father to His children.*

## 2. An Unrenewed Mind (Romans 12:1–2)

An unrenewed mind is a mind that lacks the knowledge of God's
Word. A lack of knowledge about the Word keeps us from maturing spiritually. We must ask ourselves on a regular basis, "Am I
maturing spiritually, or am I on the same level of spirituality I was
last year?" If we are not maturing, we are stagnant. At some point
in time, children have to learn how to communicate with those
around them. They can't gurgle and coo all their lives. The same
concept is true with God's children. There comes a time in the lives
of all Believers when we must study the Word more intensely in
order to discover greater revelation that will strengthen our faith.

Just as it's impossible for a child to learn English without first
being constantly exposed to it, it is also impossible for a Believer
to mature without being exposed to the deeper truths of the
Gospel. We must learn how to "speak" God's language in order
to mature and receive all that He has for us. We grow spiritually
through worship and prayer, and studying God's Word. The Word
propels us to greater levels in God.

*We must learn how to "speak" God's language in*
*order to mature and receive all that He has for us.*

## 3. Unforgiveness

Hard soil is difficult to plow and impossible to sow seed into.
That's exactly how God perceives us when we refuse to let go of

past hurts. We're deceived if we believe we can hold grudges and still expect to tune into God's frequency. Grudges create static, much like the static we hear when we are out of the range of our radio frequency.

In Matthew 6:12, Jesus prayed: "And forgive us our debts, as we forgive our debtors" (KJV). God is merciful, gracious, and just. He forgives all of our debts—whether physical, financial, spiritual, mental, or emotional. He wants us, as His beloved children, to extend forgiveness to others. In counseling sessions, I've had people say, "But Pastor Dollar, you don't know what they *did* to me!" To that I say, "It really doesn't matter! Holding on to unforgiveness is like drinking poison and hoping the individual who offended you will die!" It also opens the door for tormenting spirits to invade our lives. Those spirits cause low self-esteem, oppression, and rejection, bringing us to the lowest levels of life. Those spirits also feed off of the negativity we harbor in our hearts. That negativity tunes us in to Satan's frequency and turns up the volume. Knowing this, why would we even dare to hold a grudge against someone? It's just not worth it.

I know there are people who can really hurt us and leave us wounded. However, God can heal us and make us whole again when we trust Him. Besides, He gives us the grace to bear all things. We must learn to let go and let God.

## Take the Time to Hear Him

How many times do we go through our day making decisions instead of allowing God to tell us what He would like us to do in each situation? How often do we make decisions based on emotions rather than on the wisdom of God? Communing with God is never a waste of time. In fact, it is the best use of our time, because it enables us to tap into greater levels of His power and revelation. Hearing from God enables us to endure when we are right in the middle of difficulty. When it looks like our situations are impossible, it is our confidence in our relationship with God that brings us through. Knowing that it only takes one Word from Him to bring us victory makes our trials seem small. His grace enables us to hold on to His Word, despite the severity of the situation.

> *Hearing from God enables us to endure when we are right in the middle of difficulty.*

I had to hold on to the Word I received from God to build the Dome debt free. At first, I thought I'd missed it. I thought, *How could I do this without borrowing money?* So I tried to borrow the $17 million we needed. However, I couldn't get a loan. Then God spoke to me again, confirming what He had initially told me to do—build the Dome debt free! It seemed impossible. However, our World Dome is a testimony of God's provision.

When we hear a Word *from* the Lord, it changes us forever. Just consider Peter's life when he received a revelation from God. In Matthew chapter 16, Jesus asked His disciples who they thought He was. Peter was the only one who had the revelation knowledge to answer Him correctly. He said, "Thou art the Christ, the Son of the living God." Jesus answered and said, "Blessed art thou, Simon Bar-jona: for flesh and blood hath not revealed it unto thee, but my Father which is in heaven. And I say also unto thee, That thou art Peter, and upon this rock I will build my church; and the gates of hell shall not prevail against it" (Matthew 16:16–18 KJV). In other words, Jesus gave Peter the ability to succeed in anything he put his hand to. Why? Because he did not just shout out answers like the rest of the disciples; instead, he paused to receive new revelation from God.

Here are a few things we can do to position ourselves to hear God's voice.

## 1. Expect to Hear Him

Spending time with God will fuel our expectations. For example, when we wake up in the morning, we should imagine God's presence being there with us in the room. We should begin to talk to Him just as we would talk to someone we can see. Think about this for a moment. We talk to the people we live with all the time and we expect them to talk to us, because we can see them. On the other hand, just because we cannot see God does not mean He isn't there. For example, you can't see your brain, but you know you have one. Nor can we see the radio waves needed to pick up our favorite radio stations, but we believe they are there. We interact with things we cannot see daily. So why do we often ignore God? He's there waiting for us to speak to Him, just as we speak to our friends and loved ones.

*Spending time with God will fuel our expectations.*

There may be people in our lives who do not speak to us because they are upset about something we've said or done. However, that is not true of God. If we are not hearing from Him, it is not because He is angry at us. Folks, we have to get rid of sin-consciousness because God has sworn that He will never be angry with us. Isaiah 54:9–10 says, *"For this is like the days of Noah to Me; as I swore that the waters of Noah should no more go over the earth, so have I sworn that I will not be angry with you or rebuke you. For though the mountains should depart and the hills be shaken or removed, yet My love and kindness shall not depart from you, nor shall My covenant of peace and completeness be removed, says the Lord, Who has compassion on you."*

God has compassion for us and forgives us when we miss the mark (Hebrews 8:12). We just have to talk to Him. He wants us to turn away from our sins, because they open the door for Satan to come in and operate in our lives.

Just as God spoke to men and women in the Bible, He speaks to us today. His Word does not lie. God *wants* to speak to us. He is not holding a grudge against us. He is waiting for us to position ourselves to hear His voice, which is often small and still (1 Kings 19:12).

---

*Just as God spoke to men and women in the Bible,*
*He speaks to us today.*

---

Also, we don't have to sound superreligious when we talk to God. We must get rid of doubt and religious thinking when we spend time with Him. We don't have to come to Him repeating or screaming prayers that are long and boring, or with a list of goody-goody things we have done in order for Him to communicate with us. We do not have to "qualify" before we can speak to and hear from God. We simply approach Him with expectation and boldness, knowing He is loving and merciful and willing to help us (Hebrews 4:16).

## 2. Pray in the Spirit without Ceasing

People who do not believe in speaking in tongues may find this difficult. However, Romans 8:26 tells us that the Holy Spirit prays for and through us with words we cannot understand. Just because the natural mind can't understand our prayers in other tongues doesn't mean they aren't effective. Praying in the Spirit is more powerful than a prayer spoken in our natural language, because the Holy Spirit knows exactly what to pray at all times.

Paul commanded us in 1 Thessalonians 5:17 to pray without ceasing. To pray without ceasing means we do not neglect prayer. It means we don't forget to talk to God after our prayer time. We can talk to Him at all times—while driving to and from work or while walking up and down the halls of our schools or jobs. Our time with Him is not limited.

## 3. Boldly Obey

There's no point in hearing from God if we won't obey Him. Many times God tells us things in order to take us from one level of faith to the next. But we will never get to where He wants us to be if we do not surrender ourselves to Him. That's what the Bible calls true humility—complete and total submission to God's plan. Hebrews 11:6 tells us that God rewards those who diligently seek Him. He desires to bless us when we boldly step out in faith and trust Him at all costs. Bold obedience to God isn't always easy, but He gives us the grace to do what we can't do on our own.

*He desires to bless us when we boldly step out in faith and trust Him at all costs.*

# Life Application

Take time to review this chapter. As you do, be sure to listen for God's voice as you read certain lines. Use the following space to write down anything He is telling you to do right now. Be sure *not* to rush this step. Just slow down, listen, and write what you believe He is saying to you.

_____

_____

_____

_____

_____

_____

_____

_____

# HOW DO I KNOW WHEN I HAVE HEARD?

3

In all your ways know, recognize, *and* acknowledge Him, and He will direct *and* make straight *and* plain your paths.

—PROVERBS 3:6

To everything there is a season, and a time for every matter *or* purpose under heaven...

—ECCLESIASTES 3:1

And let us not lose heart *and* grow weary *and* faint in acting nobly *and* doing right, for in due time *and* at the appointed season we shall reap, if we do not loosen *and* relax our courage *and* faint.

—GALATIANS 6:9

But be doers of the Word [obey the message], and not merely listeners to it, betraying yourselves [into deception by reasoning contrary to the Truth].

—JAMES 1:22

In this chapter, I want to begin with a testimony that illustrates the reason I'm writing this book. I cannot emphasize enough the importance of being able to recognize God's voice. Here's the testimony of a person who got into trouble but realized the mistake before it was too late.

## Financial Breakthrough Testimony

*Dear Pastor Dollar,*

*In February, I believed God had given me permission to write checks that were not covered by sufficient funds in the bank. I believed by faith that the funds would be provided. That same day, on your television program, you said that this type of faith was foolishness. At that point, I lost faith and became frightened. I began to pray, although I believed you were wrong concerning what I had done.*

*Well, you were right. The checks I wrote were returned to me and stamped "insufficient funds." I hurriedly got all of the checks covered.*

*I continued to believe and to sow seeds toward debt cancellation. I forgave $4,000 worth of debt and, as a result, had a $14,000 debt cancelled on my rental property.*

*I thank Jesus for your ministry, and I pray for it daily. May*
*God continue to bless your ministry, members, and family.*

*P. D.*

*Salem, Oregon*

Unfortunately, many Christians have made bad financial decisions, sincerely believing they had heard from God. God doesn't lead us to error or destruction. In order to know His voice, we must spend time with Him. God has promised in His Word that He will help us to develop a relationship with Him. He wants us to know Him personally. God explained His new covenant to us as Believers:

*And it will nevermore be necessary for each one to teach his neighbor and his fellow citizen or each one his brother, saying Know (perceive, have knowledge of, and get acquainted by experience with) the Lord; for all will know Me, from the smallest to the greatest of them. For I will be merciful and gracious toward their sins and I will remember their deeds of unrighteousness no more. When God speaks of a new [covenant or agreement], He makes the first one obsolete (out of use). And what is obsolete (out of use and annulled because of age) is ripe for disappearance and to be dispensed with altogether.*

(HEBREWS 8:11–13)

We can think of a bad decision as a detour, but we cannot condemn ourselves for our mistakes. For instance, maybe you got in debt, thinking you heard from God, but now you can't pay the debt. Or maybe you wrote some bad checks (or "faith checks") that landed you in jail. Now you feel foolish for making those bad decisions. However, it won't do any good to beat yourself up over your mistakes.

Knowing how to hear the voice of God is one of the most important elements of Christian living. Why? Because God's voice provides the guidance and wisdom we need to get us from where we are now to where we want to be. John tells us in 1 John 4:1 not to believe everything we hear but to test the spirits speaking to us. Satan can appear as an angel of light (2 Corinthians 11:14) and will do anything he can to get you out of the will of God, including feeding you false information.

> *Knowing how to hear the voice of God is one of the most important elements of Christian living.*

Our inability to hear and recognize the voice of God prevents us from taking advantage of every spiritual and earthly blessing found in His Word. Simply put, we can miss our opportunity to be blessed because we are not spiritually tuned into God's frequency. It takes only one word from God to change our lives forever, but we must learn how to recognize His voice.

## His Sheep Hear His Voice

Jesus said in John 10:27, "My sheep hear my voice, and I know them, and they follow me" (KJV). The more time we spend with the Lord, the more we will be able to recognize His voice, just as sheep recognize the voice of their shepherd. If we don't know who's speaking to us, we will follow any voice we hear, and we open ourselves to all kinds of deceiving spirits. The bottom line is, we can hear either from God or from the devil, but only one voice will lead us to real victory. We must establish ourselves as God's hearing sheep.

Sheep are vulnerable creatures. In the Bible, shepherds cared for them, thereby spending a considerable amount of time with them. The sheep learned to depend on the shepherd to provide their daily needs and to protect them from harm. Because of this daily fellowship and interaction, these animals became just as familiar with the shepherd as a child is with his or her mother.

Likewise, as our Father, God provides for us and guides us through our human spirits, which is the very core of us. We must pay attention to the hunches or inner impressions we have about a particular situation. If we have spent quality time in God's Word and prayed in the Spirit, we can trust those inward leadings. His Word says to acknowledge Him in all our ways, and He will direct our path (Proverbs 3:6).

---

*We must pay attention to the hunches or inner impressions we have about a particular situation.*

---

When we have questions about whether we have heard from God, we should allow the peace of God to determine if we should proceed or not. This is when the Holy Spirit testifies with our spirits that something is right or wrong. We cannot afford to ignore these "checks" in our spirits. Again, the ability to recognize God's voice comes from spending time with Him.

## Recognizing the Wrong Voice

What do you do when you want to hear a particular radio station or type of music? More than likely you hit a button that selects the station you want to hear. The key is in knowing what to listen for. If the wrong type of music comes on, you know you have the wrong station. That's the way it is with God. If you hear something that does not line up with His Word, it's not His voice. His voice is like a signal, and we tune our ears to His frequency.

Many people think hearing from God is "deep" or "spooky." However, learning to hear His voice should be a part of our daily lives as Christians. If you believe you have received a Word from God, the next step is to be sure you heard from God before you step out. Follow these seven procedures to test what you have heard.

## 1. Submit the Issue to Christ's Lordship

As the Lord of your life, God knows how to bless you. Desire and honor His plans for you above anything else.

## 2. Believe that God Will Speak to You

God wants to speak to you; only believe (Mark 1:40–41). Eliminate all questioning and doubt. Pay attention to the voice of your conscience. God will also speak to you sometimes in impressions (a song, a person, a sermon, or a hunch).

## 3. Listen as God Transmits His Word into Your Spirit

The Spirit of truth will transmit His Word to you (John 16:13–14).

## 4. Learn How to Test What You Have Heard

If what you have heard is not based in unconditional love, and does not line up perfectly with the Word, it didn't come from God

(Psalm 119:4–5; 24). If it does not exalt, glorify, and magnify Jesus, it did not come from God. If it brings confusion, condemnation, or discouragement, disregard it (1 Corinthians 14:33; James 3:13–17). If what you have heard does not line up with these safeguards, chances are you did *not* hear from God at all.

## 5. Seek Godly Counsel

Do not seek yes men and yes women. Choose someone who will tell you the truth.

Proverbs 13:20 tells us that he who walks with the wise becomes wise. Sometimes we allow our own emotions to blind us to warning signs that may be present in our situations. The only remedy for that is to seek the counsel of Believers who have proven themselves to be mature by the fruit they bear. Do not seek the counsel of an immature Believer or an unsaved person, because neither has sufficient experience in dealing with the things of God. Seek counsel from those who can confirm God's voice to you through the Word of God.

## 6. Wait for God's Timing. He Will Tell You How and When.

For everything there is a due season (Ecclesiastes 3:1). To avoid frustration and the temptation to quit, understand there is a due season for you (Galatians 6:9). Continue to do what God last told you to do; continue to sow (Ecclesiastes 11:1–4).

## 7. Take Action!

When hearing from God, be willing to obey God. Be a doer of the Word (James 1:21–22). The Word you hear will require faith and courage. It will always line up with God's Word, it will often go against the reasons and rationalizations of the world, and peace will rule in your heart like an umpire.

Follow peace. Allow the peace of God to rule in your heart before making a decision. This is when the Holy Spirit testifies with your spirit that something is either wrong or right. If it's right, you'll experience peace. If it is wrong, there will be an absence of peace. Remember the devil will use every opportunity to deceive you if he thinks he can. Wait for the peace of God to confirm what you've heard. If you have any "funny feelings," it's the Holy Spirit letting you know that what you heard was *not* the voice of God.

# Life Application

Since everything in the kingdom of God requires faith, here are some declarations you can make daily that will stir up your faith and help you hear God's voice more clearly.

## Daily Confessions

### *Hearing from God*

- *Heavenly Father, I declare that I possess a hearing heart. I hear from You in specific detail, not in vague impressions. Every word I hear from You empowers me to prosper and excel.*

- *I stand firm in You, Lord. Because I am established in righteousness, the gates of hell do not prevail against me. Speak to me concerning what I need to do to live for You and experience the reality of Your blessings in my life. I obey You in all things; therefore, Your Word always comes to pass in my life.*

- *I am Your sheep, and You are my Shepherd. I know Your voice, and the voice of a stranger I do not follow. I hear Your voice clearly and obey immediately. In Jesus' name, amen!*

# THE HOLY SPIRIT AS
# A FINANCIAL ADVISOR

4

But the person who is united to the Lord
becomes one spirit with Him.

—1 CORINTHIANS 6:17

Beloved, do not put faith in every spirit, but prove
(test) the spirits to discover whether they proceed
from God; for many false prophets have gone
forth into the world.

—1 JOHN 4:1

So too the [Holy] Spirit comes to our aid *and*
bears us up in our weakness; for we do not know
what prayer to offer *nor* how to offer it worthily
as we ought, but the Spirit Himself goes to meet
our supplication *and* pleads in our behalf with
unspeakable yearnings *and* groanings too deep
for utterance.

—ROMANS 8:26

As a young couple, Taffi and I struggled for years just to make ends meet. We had student loans, car notes, rent, monthly utilities, and credit card bills to pay. After we paid all those bills, we barely had enough to survive until the next paycheck. When we had children, we realized we needed miraculous help, because we were living way beyond our means. Our income was no match for our growing debt. I knew we needed God's guidance to get out of the financial mess we were in. I began to seek God for wisdom.

During that time, God called me into ministry to preach the Word of God with simplicity and understanding to the body of Christ. It seemed challenging to answer this great call while I was experiencing financial bondage. Nevertheless, I answered the call. I'm so glad I didn't have to depend on my own efforts to make it through my financial difficulties. I learned to depend on the guidance of the Holy Spirit.

Although I began to rely on the leading of the Holy Spirit concerning my finances, I knew I had a part to play in gaining total financial freedom. I knew I couldn't rely on God to do everything while I sat idly and watched. No, I had to act in faith and make the necessary adjustments. Taffi and I had to break the habits that were causing us financial problems. For instance, we had to stop spending beyond our means. We had to learn how to trim our everyday living expenses significantly and live on a budget.

*We had to learn how to trim our everyday living
expenses significantly and live on a budget.*

Taffi and I both worked in order to pay off the debt. I even worked overtime to earn extra money to pay off our debt. We also had to maintain our decision to stop getting further into debt. We started making good financial decisions while relying on the Holy Spirit to help us along the way. And He did! He gave us favor, witty ideas and concepts, supernatural debt cancellation, and much more. It wasn't an overnight process, however. As we developed spiritually and matured in wise decision making, we were able to get out of financial bondage and stay out.

Through the study of God's Word and the ministry of the Holy Spirit, we were able to become debt free and stay free. The Holy Spirit led us to the teachings of men and women who I believe are generals on the subject of total life prosperity. We began to tap into the wisdom we had within by confessing the Word of God daily. Eventually, our mind-set changed. We really began to believe that God wanted us to succeed financially. I am so glad I surrendered to Him and decided to trust Him instead of my efforts alone.

I am convinced that God does not want Christians to suffer financial bondage. This is why we have His Word and His way of doing things. Sadly, many Christians do not read the Word to find out His good plans for them. His precious promises are not ancient news; they are living words packed with His power. In order for our deliverance to take place, we have to believe the Word of God and trust in the guidance of the Holy Spirit. When we follow the leadership of the Holy Spirit, we'll discover that

He not only wants to lead us out of financial bondage but other bondages we may be trapped in as well.

---

*In order for our deliverance to take place,*
*we have to believe the Word of God and trust*
*in the guidance of the Holy Spirit.*

---

## Acknowledging the Spiritual Realm

The Barna Group recently reported that "among those who believe they are Christians, just one-fifth say they live in a way that makes them completely dependent on God." The research also indicated that only "one-sixth of Christians say they are totally committed to engaging in personal spiritual development."[2]

We have been conditioned to believe only in what we can see, hear, touch, and smell; however, we must not forget a spiritual realm exists that determines what happens in the physical realm. All physical things originated in the unseen, spiritual realm, including mankind. We should keep in mind that we are spirits living in physical bodies, and the spiritual things we cannot see are just as real as the physical things we *can* see.

Man is a tripartite being—spirit, soul, and body (1 Thessalonians 5:23). The body can be contacted with physical things, and the soul can be contacted with words. However, the spirit of a person cannot be contacted by anything in this natural, physical realm. The only way to contact the spirit is through the Word of God.

Our born-again spirit is one with God; it is as perfect, mature, and complete as Jesus is (Hebrews 12:23). We are joined with the

Holy Spirit. We are one with Him (1 Corinthians 6:17). How-ever, we must maintain an awareness of the Holy Spirit's presence within us in order to tap into the divine power we possess.

## Knowing Our Unseen Partner

Getting to know someone intimately takes time. For example, before a man and woman consider marriage, they, more than likely, have spent quality time together building trust and learn-ing about each other. Likewise, in order to build trust and know our unseen partner, we must spend quality time with Him through prayer and reading the Word. According to 1 Corinthians 6:19, our bodies are "temples of the Holy Ghost" (KJV). He lives on the inside of us because He wants to be a part of *everything* we do. It is not His desire to sit idly by and watch our lives unfold with-out getting involved. If we position ourselves to hear His voice, He will reveal God's perfect plan for our lives.

*If we position ourselves to hear His voice,*
*He will reveal God's perfect plan for our lives.*

Although the Holy Spirit lives on the inside of us, we don't automatically get to know Him and His ways. That will take time, focus, and engagement. That is why it is so important for us to study the Word of God. By doing so, we learn to recognize not only His voice but also His character and nature. In addition, we have to learn to communicate with the Holy Spirit. For example, if there's no communication between a husband and wife, their relationship becomes mechanical. Although they may share the same home, they simply coexist. Unfortunately, this is true for many Christians and their relationship with the Holy Spirit. They are aware of His presence, yet they merely coexist with the Holy Spirit, failing to communicate with Him. As a result, they don't receive answers to the everyday dilemmas they find themselves in. As with any relationship, our relationship with the Holy Spirit will weaken without constant communication.

Prayer is a wonderful way to communicate with the Holy Spirit. However, prayer is not a monologue. It is a dialogue. We must not do all the talking. It is important to listen for God to speak back to us. We can also pray mysteries by speaking in the spirit as the Holy Spirit gives us utterance. This is the gift of praying in tongues. Regardless of whether we pray in our natural language or in tongues, prayer is a vital part of developing a relationship with the Holy Spirit.

---

*Prayer is a wonderful way to communicate with the Holy Spirit.*

---

## Where Are You Going?

I like to think of the Holy Spirit as a spiritual tour guide. He provides the specific directions on how to get from point A to point B in God's perfect will for our lives. He knows the exact route we need to take and the amount of time it will take us to get there. He's already aware of the forks in the road and the detours. Many of life's frustrating detours can be avoided by simply seeking Him and obeying His voice.

We all have times in our lives when we are not sure which direction we should take. That's why it helps to know the Holy Spirit intimately. He will lead us in fulfilling God's perfect plan for our lives. Within His plan, we will have all the resources we need, including the finances to get out of debt and to live without lack.

There are many great examples of God-fearing men and women who were led by the Holy Spirit in the book of Acts of the Apostles. For instance, a group of God-fearing men at the church of Antioch were seeking God for direction concerning the work of the ministry. The Bible tells us: *"One day as these men were worshiping the Lord and fasting, the Holy Spirit said, 'Dedicate Barnabas and Saul for the special work to which I have called them.' So after more fasting and prayer, the men laid their hands on them and sent them on their way. So Barnabas and Saul were sent out by the Holy Spirit. They went down to the seaport of Seleucia and then sailed for the island of Cyprus. There, in the town of Salamis, they went to the Jewish synagogues and preached the word of God"* (Acts 13:2–5 NLT).

These men could have tried casting lots for direction rather than taking the time to seek God for answers. They didn't get caught up in their busy schedules; instead, they yielded themselves to their unseen partner. Likewise, we all have busy schedules—family, friends, leisure activities—that compete for our time. However, we must put first things first and schedule everything else around spending time with the Holy Spirit on a daily basis so we can receive direction. I usually get up early in the morning, before the dew settles, to spend time with the Holy Spirit, not just to seek him for financial guidance, but to know Him intimately. It all boils down to having a relationship with a loving God who wants to give us the answers we need to live the good life He has planned for us.

*We must put first things first and schedule everything else around spending time with the Holy Spirit on a daily basis so we can receive direction.*

I can't stress enough the importance of becoming proficient in recognizing and hearing His voice clearly, because there are many imitations (1 John 4:1). If you're not careful, you might listen to the wrong voice and get off course. Isaiah 42:16 says, "And I will bring the blind by a way that they knew not; I will lead them in paths that they have not known: I will make darkness light before them, and crooked things straight. These things will I do unto them, and not forsake them" (KJV). In this Scripture, God is not talking about leading those who are physically blind but those who are spiritually blind. When we become familiar with His voice, it is easy to follow His instructions.

The Holy Spirit is a champion at *giving* us sweatless victory. We don't have to beg God to meet our needs. He has already met them; it is included in His plan for our lives. Jesus assured us that when we seek first the kingdom of God and His righteousness, everything else—debt freedom, prosperity, healing—will manifest (Matthew 6:33). He has already provided everything we will ever need.

God gives us the ability to fulfill His plan for our lives. That ability to walk confidently on the path He places us on is a direct result of the wisdom that comes from the Holy Spirit. His wisdom chases away confusion and equips us for success, gives us divine insight into the Word, and helps us accept His promises as reality.

*God gives us the ability to fulfill His plan for our lives.*

## Allow Him to Take the Lead

God doesn't want us accepting everything life throws at us without a clue as to how to respond. He not only wants to be involved, but He also wants to have a leadership position in our lives. By giving us His Spirit to dwell in us, God has given us the answer to every problem we will ever face in life. However, it is only through an intimate relationship with the Holy Spirit that we receive the answers to our problems. He is our helper. He's ready, willing, and able to help us in our weaknesses, and He makes intercession for us (Romans 8:26). He will be there whenever we need Him.

I pray you have gained a deeper understanding of the important role the Holy Spirit plays in our lives. If you are struggling to get out of debt or financial bondage, I encourage you to seek Him for wisdom and answers to your financial challenges. Allow Him to fulfill His ministry through you. If you do, He will order your steps as you develop a more intimate relationship with Him. Additionally, He will speak and reveal God's will for your life. Remember, He is your silent partner who wants to lead you each step of the way. The question is, will you let Him?

# Life Application

Are you struggling to make ends meet? Does it seem that nothing is working in your life? If so, I want you to begin to pray, acknowledging the Holy Spirit's presence within you. Then give Him time to speak to you. If you're not sure you are hearing *His* voice, take a moment to listen. Remember, prayer should not be a mechanical, one-way line of communication—it's a dialogue between you and God. When you finish your time in prayer today, write down what He says to you. Write down any Scripture He brings to your mind. Then, throughout the day, refer to your notes, thanking Him for the wisdom and revelation you received.

# WISDOM: THE 5 KEY INGREDIENT TO FINANCIAL SUCCESS

If any of you is deficient in wisdom, let him
ask of the giving God [Who gives] to everyone
liberally *and* ungrudgingly, without reproaching
*or* faultfinding, and it will be given him.

—JAMES 1:5

For I [Myself] will give you a mouth *and* such
utterance and wisdom that all of your foes
combined will be unable to stand against or
refute.

—LUKE 21:15

Saying in a loud voice, Deserving is the Lamb,
Who was sacrificed, to receive all the power and
riches and wisdom and might and honor and
majesty (glory, splendor) and blessing!

—REVELATION 5:12

When I was a child, my mother used to make apple pies from scratch. Before she began, she would gather all of the ingredients together: salt, sugar, water, apples, cinnamon, and flour. She followed the recipe, and as a result, her pies always came out perfectly. If she had not followed the recipe and tried to substitute the apples with oranges, the pies would have been disasters. She knew the only way to produce delicious, edible treats was to use the right ingredients and follow the instructions.

## Getting out of Debt and Gaining Financial Freedom

God's way is similar to baking an apple pie. We must first have the recipe in front of us—the Word of God—in order to know what is needed and how to put it all together to get the results we desire. And just as an apple is the main ingredient in apple pie, wisdom is the key ingredient to receiving godly financial advice and deliverance. In fact, wisdom unlocks the door to anything we need in life. It is the answer to every problem, question, situation, and circumstance we encounter. By obtaining it, we can overcome any obstacle in our path and receive God's abundance.

*Wisdom unlocks the door to anything we need in life.*

## A Facet of the Anointing (or Empowerment)

Wisdom is one of the most important characteristics of the Holy Spirit mentioned in Isaiah 11:2: "And the spirit of the Lord shall rest upon him, the spirit of wisdom and understanding, the spirit of counsel and might, the spirit of knowledge and of the fear of the Lord" (KJV). In other words, wisdom is part of the burden-removing, yoke-destroying power of God—the same power that operated through Jesus and is in us today. It gives direction and provides guidance. And by operating in this empowerment, we can experience deliverance from financial bondage. We no longer have to work out our deliverance from debt in our own strength or with the limited knowledge of the world. Instead, by grace through faith, God can and will help us unravel our financial challenges. However, it will take effort on our part, which consists of placing our complete trust in Him while carrying out His instructions. We must operate by faith and not by what we see.

*By grace through faith, God can and will help us unravel our financial challenges.*

Before we can obtain wisdom, we must have a good understanding of what wisdom really is. Contrary to what we may think, wisdom is *not* just knowledge. Wisdom is revelation knowledge that comes from God. His wisdom *illuminates* the knowledge we have and gives us divine direction. For example, we can study the Pythagorean theorem until we're blue in the face, but unless we know how to use it in our everyday lives, it does us no good. Knowledge that is revealed by the Almighty comes with instruction that exceeds anything we can find in the world.

Jesus understood and operated according to this principle. For instance, Mark 6:35–43 (KJV) reveals what happened when He fed five thousand people:

> *And when the day was now far spent, his disciples came unto him, and said, This is a desert place, and now the time is far passed: Send them away, that they may go into the country round about, and into the villages, and buy themselves bread: for they have nothing to eat. He answered and said unto them, Give ye them to eat. And they say unto him, Shall we go and buy two hundred pennyworth of bread, and give them to eat? He saith unto them, How many loaves have ye? Go and see. And when they knew, they say, Five, and two fishes. And he commanded them to make all sit down by companies upon the green grass. And they sat down in ranks, by hundreds, and by fifties. And when he had taken the five loaves and the two fishes, he looked up to heaven, and blessed, and brake the loaves, and gave them to his disciples to set before them; and the two fishes divided he among them all. And they all did eat, and were filled. And they took up twelve baskets full of the fragments, and of the fishes.*

It's worth noting that the disciples had enough common sense to realize that they did not have enough food to feed everyone standing on the shore that day. However, this basic knowledge of the situation was not enough to solve the problem. That was when the anointing of wisdom kicked in. Instead of panicking or whining over the situation, Jesus took the two-piece fish dinner, blessed it, and then passed it around. As a result, over five thousand people were fed, and there was enough left over to fill twelve baskets!

Now, take a moment to imagine what the disciples must have thought when Jesus told them to command the people to sit down. From a human perspective, they didn't have nearly enough food to feed the large crowd. By mere knowledge, they could conclude only that it was best to send the people away to get food. However, contrary to their "common sense," Jesus did something out of the ordinary—He blessed the food. Jesus knew the wisdom of God would seem foolish to His disciples, who were operating according to mere human or worldly common sense (1 Corinthians 1:25). Blessing the food probably didn't make sense to them. Therefore, Jesus didn't try to explain it to them. Instead, He showed them how to operate in wisdom by praying, stepping out in faith, and believing that God would meet the needs of the people. Jesus blessed the food, and the food was multiplied. Everyone there saw the manifestation of the glory of God!

*Jesus knew the wisdom of God would seem foolish to His disciples.*

## God's Word Is Wisdom

Wisdom is not some unattainable force floating around in the atmosphere. It is an anointing—a part of the Holy Spirit—that lives inside every born-again Believer. We have everything that is a part of Him—every characteristic, anointing, and facet of His personality. He is the "initial deposit" who guarantees our inheritance of salvation, or *soteria*—protection, safety, soundness, provision, and prosperity. It's important to understand that once we possess this initial deposit of the Holy Spirit, we should not let His anointing remain dormant in our lives. On the contrary, we must learn how to tap into it and then do our best to increase that anointing. We do this through careful, diligent study of the Word of God, which is God's wisdom. In fact, we can even substitute the phrase *Word of God* for *Wisdom* anywhere in the Bible.

To get wisdom, we must get an understanding of the Word. Without understanding, we won't recognize when the Word of God speaks specifically to our circumstances. As a result, we will be unable to apply the Word to our daily lives. This is why I preach in a way that is simple and comprehensive. It does my congregation no good to sit and listen to a great-sounding sermon and not learn how to apply it to evoke change in their lives. Further, in order for them to mature spiritually, they must fully understand the Word.

---

*To get wisdom, we must get an understanding of the Word.*

---

Proverbs 4:5–7 commands us to get wisdom and understanding because wisdom is the principal, or most important, thing. Without it, we cannot obtain the blessings of God. Wisdom—the Word of God—shows us exactly what we need to do to receive those blessings. But it does more than that—it promotes, protects, and gives life. Wisdom leads us down the path God has predestined us to take. It's a path without regrets—not that we won't have any challenges along the way. But by aligning ourselves with the Word of God, we prepare the way for wisdom to operate through and for us. The Bible assures us that when this happens, no one will be able to resist the words that come out of our mouths (Luke 21:15). When we speak and live by the Word of God, we speak and live by wisdom.

Solomon had firsthand knowledge of this principle. First Kings 3:3–9 tells us that when he was crowned king after the death of his father, David, he prayed not for wealth and favor but for an "understanding" heart. He knew there was no way to successfully govern God's people without wisdom. As a result, his simple request pleased God so much that He gave Solomon more than what he asked for. Not only was Solomon blessed with wisdom but also with wealth beyond measure: *"Behold,...I have given thee a wise and an understanding heart; so that there was none like thee before thee, neither after thee shall any arise like unto thee. And I have also given thee...riches, and honour: so that there shall not be any among the kings like unto thee all thy days"* (1 Kings 3:12–13 KJV).

Solomon's wealth and wisdom did not come without a sacrifice. He sowed for it. In fact, the Bible tells us he gave one thousand burned offerings and received a hundred times more than what he asked for (1 Kings 3:4, 10–13; 1 Kings 10:23). That in itself was a form of wisdom in operation. Solomon was fully aware that he needed favor with God, and that the way to get it was to humble himself before the Lord prior to making his request known. He simply followed the example of his father, who said, *"neither will I offer burnt offerings unto the Lord my God of that which doth cost me nothing"* (2 Samuel 24:24 KJV). As a result of his integrity and desire to please God, Solomon received the answer to his request that very night in a dream (1 Kings 3:5).

---

*Solomon's wealth and wisdom did not come without a sacrifice.*

---

## A Valuable Asset

The kingdom of God works by the principle of seedtime and harvest found in Galatians 6:7. The principle is symbolically based on the way in which a farmer sows seed into the ground and produces a greater harvest. Today, in all that we do, we should keep in mind that God's principle of sowing and reaping is still in operation. Solomon's sacrificial offering got God's attention (2 Chronicles 1:3-12). Solomon's attitude—his willingness to do what was necessary to obtain the wisdom of God—pleased God. He "sowed" a great seed and produced a greater harvest.

Obtaining the wisdom of God must become a way of life for us as Believers. We never know when we are going to need to tap into that wisdom. Therefore, we can't wait until the last minute to effectively operate in wisdom. Learning to operate in wisdom takes time and development. For example, several years ago, one of my employees stole over ten thousand dollars from the ministry. What bothered me most was the fact that the television bill was due in a few days, and because of what this employee had done, it looked as if we would not be able to pay the bill. Immediately my mind began to think of ways to get the money back. But God had another plan in mind.

*Obtaining the wisdom of God must become a*
*way of life for us as Believers.*

After I finally sought God for direction, He spoke to my heart and told me exactly what I needed to do. He took me to a couple of Scriptures (Matthew 6:12; Luke 6:37) to prepare my heart for what He wanted me to do. The instructions were as simple: forgive the man of the offense, call the television stations to explain the situation, and ask for an extension. To be honest, that was difficult to do. From an emotional standpoint, I really wanted to make that man return what he had stolen—with interest! But, instead, I chose the better way and yielded myself to the wisdom of God regardless of how I felt. As a result of my obedience and willingness to forgive, every station manager I called that day waived the television bill for that month. In the end, I reaped more than I lost! Glory to God! Wisdom—God's Word—had instructed me and provided a way out of the situation.

## Don't Reject Wisdom

What would have happened if I had rejected the wisdom of God concerning the ten thousand dollars that was stolen? More than likely I would not be on the air as much as I am today. You see, I didn't wait until the last minute to cultivate a relationship with God. I didn't wait until the last minute to gain knowledge of His Word. The ability to hear from God and operate in His wisdom comes only by spending time with Him on a daily basis. That is how Jesus Himself was able to operate in wisdom. If you study the Scriptures carefully, you'll discover that Jesus' life was a pattern of prayer and miracles. He did and said nothing apart from the Father. Every word He spoke was the wisdom of God (John 12:49–50; John 5:19).

In addition to giving divine direction, wisdom gives us knowledge that is not found in the world. For example, since the economy began to decline in 2007, a growing number of people were unable to find suitable employment. Many of those people included college graduates. Despite their level of education, the school they attended, or how well they did in school, many graduates in recent years have had a difficult time finding jobs. In some cases, those who did find jobs found that their work didn't even require a college degree. I've seen people who have dropped out of high school use godly wisdom to devise a successful business plan and operate a successful business. They didn't have the impressive degrees to rely on or any type of knowledge that would be acceptable in society. However, God gave them the wisdom to develop a successful company. God's instruction to us at times may be surprising. His divine instructions may go against worldly wisdom, but it lines up perfectly with His Word. For example, He may tell you to call someone who owes you money and forgive them of the debt. Well, that's a seed sown. You'll no doubt get more from that harvest than you would if the person had given you the money. We must learn to rely on God's wisdom because His way is always the best way.

---

*God's instruction to us at times may be surprising.*

---

## Wisdom at Work

Wisdom can give us witty ideas. According to worldly (or society's) standards, we may not have all the credentials that are typically regarded as necessary to be successful, but that shouldn't stop us. What the world says pales in comparison to what God says. The Word of God says that He is a God of witty inventions (Proverbs 8:12). His Word is the final authority.

When we are operating in true, godly wisdom, everyone around us knows. Godly wisdom can be seen. That was how the Queen of Sheba came to know about Solomon's wisdom. She had heard about his wealth and wisdom and came to *see* it for herself. And what she saw made her faint (1 Kings 10:4–7).

Wisdom produces wealth, just like cooking produces an aroma of delicious food. Wisdom can bring forth riches (Psalm 104:24), produce witty inventions (Proverbs 8:12), and cause everything we do to multiply. With benefits like these, why would anyone want to turn away from wisdom? That's like a person who falls into a pit and refuses to climb a ladder to escape! It just doesn't make sense to refuse a God-given method for success. The God-kind of debt deliverance comes by applying the principles of wisdom only. That is why we must make a quality decision to turn away from the world's system of debt cancellation and turn toward God's method of sweatless, guaranteed success. He wants us to learn to work smarter instead of harder.

*The God-kind of debt deliverance comes by applying the principles of wisdom only.*

It's important to remember that those in the Bible who experienced great success operated in the anointing of wisdom. Bezaleel and Aholiab put together the tent of meeting for the Israelites (Exodus 31:1–6). Joshua led the Israelites into the Promised Land and defeated the enemies of God (Deuteronomy 34:9). And Solomon reigned successfully over the kingdom of Israel (1 Kings 4:29) until he turned away from God's Word—the very thing that protected him from destruction.

Wisdom is the key ingredient to financial success. It illuminates the path to God's abundance, but it must be sought with the same intensity that wealth is sought. If we continually employ wisdom in our lives, we will not only obtain wealth, but we will also have the ability to *retain* it. It does us no good to get out of debt and then find ourselves in the same hole a few months or years later. Wisdom is a powerful tool designed to help us live the abundant life Jesus promised in John 10:10. But it's up to us to employ it on a daily basis. We must make a quality decision to become all God desires us to be through the anointing of wisdom.

*Wisdom is a powerful tool designed to help us live the abundant life Jesus promised in John 10:10.*

# Life Application

One way to begin to change your thinking so that it lines up with the Word is through meditation. One form of meditation is speaking something out loud repeatedly. Below are Word-based confessions that will help you operate in wisdom when dealing with your finances.

## Declarations for Finances and Debt Cancellation

- *Psalm 35:27 says God delights in the prosperity of His servants. Therefore, as His servant, I declare that I am out of debt, my needs are met, and I have plenty more to put in store.*

- *I no longer operate by the world's system of debt cancellation, but by God's system of seedtime and harvest. When I give financially, I reap an immediate, hundredfold return on whatever I give. As I give, it is given unto me, good measure—pressed down, shaken together, and running over—do men give into my bosom (Galatians 6:7, Luke 6:38).*

- *I am a cheerful giver, and I sow under the direction of the Holy Spirit (2 Corinthians 9:7).*

- *I meditate on God's Word daily. As a result, I boldly and courageously follow the Lord. I hear God's voice clearly and operate in His wisdom and anointing (Joshua 1:8—9).*

- *Proverbs 4:23 says that out of the heart flow the issues of life. Therefore, I refuse to allow anything to come before my eyes, in my ears, or out of my mouth that does not line up with the Word of God. I purpose to guard my heart diligently by bringing every thought, action, or desire into submission to the Word.*

- *God delights in my prosperity. He gives me power to get wealth so that He may establish His covenant upon the earth (Deuteronomy 8:18).*

- *God has given me all things that pertain to life and godliness, and I am well able to possess all that God has provided for me (2 Peter 1:3).*

- *God is my only Source. I put my trust in God, not in man (Jeremiah 17:5–7).*

- *My God makes all grace abound toward me in every favor and earthly blessing so that I have sufficiency for all things and abound to every good work.*

- *I renew my mind to the truth about God's desire to financially prosper me.*

- *The Lord is my shepherd, and I do not want. He came so that I may have life and have it more abundantly (Psalm 23:1; John 10:10).*

- *The spirit of truth abides in me and teaches me all things, and He guides me into all truth. Therefore, I confess that I have perfect knowledge of every situation and every circumstance that I come up against, for I have the wisdom of God now (John 16:13).*

- *I trust in the Lord with all my heart and lean not unto my own understanding. In all my ways I acknowledge Him, and He directs my paths (Proverbs 3:5–6).*

- *The Lord will perfect that which concerns me (Psalm 138:8).*

- *I do follow the good Shepherd, and I know His voice, and the voice of a stranger I will not follow (John 10:4–5).*

- *I confess that I have the wisdom of God. I am filled with the knowledge of the Lord's will in all wisdom and spiritual understanding (Colossians 1:9).*

# 6

# CHANGING A POVERTY MIND-SET

For as he thinks in his heart, so is he...

—PROVERBS 23:7A


So we built the wall, and all [of it] was joined together to half its height, for the people had a heart *and* mind to work.

—NEHEMIAH 4:6


For the drunkard and the glutton shall come to poverty, and drowsiness shall clothe a man with rags.

—PROVERBS 23:21


Honor the Lord with your capital *and* sufficiency [from righteous labors] and with the first fruits of all your income...

—PROVERBS 3:9

Grace doesn't give us an excuse to ignore God's Word or His principles for living a godly lifestyle. Although we are under grace, we must still renew our minds with the Word. Many Believers fail to begin and stick with the process of mind renewal. As such, they continue to live in poverty. Because their minds have not been renewed by the Word, they operate in the principles of poverty instead of the biblical principles of prosperity.

Poverty begins as a mind-set. Many people are living below the standard that God desires for them, and they can't break free because of the way they think. They have embraced beliefs that do not line up with the Word of God. As a result, they have positioned themselves for failure. In order to break into the life of abundance that God has promised us, it is critical that we recognize a poverty mind-set and break out of it by applying and practicing God's Word concerning prosperity.

*Many people are living below the standard that God desires for them, and they can't break free because of the way they think.*

Have you ever wondered why you think the way you do? Our beliefs are based on the information we have received about a particular subject over a period of time. That information may have come through our families, environments, friends, or traditions that have been passed down from one generation to the next. Many times we accept circumstances as "just the way things are" without realizing that God has better things intended for us. We have to challenge those beliefs that don't come from the Word.

Many people look at my current lifestyle and assume that I don't know anything about what it means to live in a poverty-stricken environment. What they fail to realize is that I had to learn God's Word about prosperity and allow it to change my thinking. I remember as a child having to eat government cheese and peanut butter because my family was struggling financially. My mother made meals and fed our whole family with minimal resources. I also recall scrubbing mildew off the walls of our home and raking a front yard full of dirt because we couldn't afford to have grass. I know what it's like to live in poverty, but thank God for His grace and mercy!

God gave me revelation about the God-kind of prosperity by leading me to men and women of God who were teaching the truth about prosperity from His Word. Through these teachings, I found my passion: teaching people how to prosper according to God's Word. I often tell my congregation that the principles I teach on prosperity have been tried and proven in my life. It was because of God's grace that I discovered His principles for living. It was by grace through faith that God delivered me from a poverty mind-set. Over a period of time, I began to see the God-kind of financial success manifest in my life.

## The Characteristics of Poverty

*Webster's Dictionary* defines *poverty* as "a chronic pressing need for money and material goods; inferior quality." The *Random House*

*Dictionary* describes *poverty* as "the state or condition of having little or no money, goods, or means of support;...deficiency;... scantiness; insufficiency." However, just as prosperity applies to more than material possessions, so does poverty. Poverty is much more than being broke financially, although financial insufficiency is an aspect of being impoverished. Poverty can also extend to our mental, physical, and spiritual well-being.

---

*Poverty can also extend to our mental, physical, and spiritual well-being.*

---

Poverty is a part of the curse, and defines deficiencies of all kinds. If something is deficient, it is lacking. A curse is the opposite of the blessing. It is an empowerment to fail. When we live in poverty, we are empowered to fail rather than to prosper. There is nothing positive or godly about poverty, despite what we may have learned growing up in our traditional religious circles. It takes the burden-removing, yoke-destroying power of God to put an end to poverty forever.

Nothing just happens. The Word of God says that a curse cannot come without a cause (Proverbs 26:2). Just as a man who is prosperous didn't become wealthy without cause, the same is true with a person who lives in poverty. Prosperity and poverty are both governed by certain principles that must be activated in order for these entities to become realities in our lives.

---

*Prosperity and poverty are both governed by certain principles that must be activated in order for these entities to become realities in our lives.*

---

The first characteristic of poverty is found in Proverbs 24:30–31. This passage talks about how laziness causes poverty: *"I went by the field of the lazy man, and by the vineyard of the man void of understanding; And, behold, it was all grown over with thorns, and nettles were covering its face, and its stone wall was broken down."* When a person has a slothful attitude, they are inviting a spirit of poverty to destroy what they have.

I want to now focus on financial poverty. I know it may be a hard truth to accept, but lazy people will never acquire lasting wealth. In order to become financially prosperous in God's system of operation, aside from renewing our minds with the Word, we must also do some things in the *natural* realm. Working hard is one of those things. Unfortunately, I've seen many Christians pray, believe, and confess the Word regarding financial increase, but when it comes to getting a job, starting their own business, or working diligently on the job they currently have, they fall short. Then they wonder why they never see any signs of financial increase. The reason is simple: they are operating in a principle of poverty, which is laziness or slothfulness.

Slothfulness can describe a person's entire approach toward life and everything he or she does. Slothful people allow things to pile up instead of staying on top of them and getting them done in a timely manner. This type of person sleeps all day, although he or she knows there are tasks that need to be completed. A slothful individual is slow to make the necessary effort to accomplish tasks successfully, which often leads to poverty.

In contrast, a diligent person works hard even without supervision. As a result, this person receives promotion from God. We have to ask ourselves questions like: "Am I a lazy or diligent person?" Furthermore, keep in mind that even when no one else sees us, God does, and He weighs what is going on in our hearts.

*A diligent person works hard even*
*without supervision.*

The second characteristic of poverty ties in with the first, which is sleeping more than necessary (Proverbs 20:13). Sleep is a natural physiological need, but sleeping beyond what the body needs is a hindrance to success. No one can be productive by sleeping most of the day and all through the night. Time should be set aside to set and accomplish goals on a daily basis. Otherwise, failure is inevitable. Even in regard to our relationship with God, we must set aside quality time for Him and His Word.

The third characteristic of poverty is stinginess. The Bible is full of Scriptures that talk about the rewards of being a giver. For instance, Proverbs 11:24 states: *"There is that scattereth, and yet increaseth; and there is that witholdeth more than is meet, but it tendeth to poverty"* (KJV). Holding on to the little we have because we fear not having enough indicates that we are operating in selfishness (the opposite of love). When we operate outside of God's system, we are cut off from His provision.

*"Give and it shall be given unto you; good measure, pressed down, and shaken together, and running over, shall men give into your bosom. For with the same measure that ye mete withal it shall be measured to you again"* (Luke 6:38). The Word makes it plain: the person who gives with a willing heart *will* receive the same and more.

Characteristic number four is found in Proverbs 13:18: *"Poverty and shame shall be to him that refuseth instruction: but he that regardeth reproof shall be honored."* People who refuse to receive instruction or correction are headed toward poverty. These people have an unteachable mind-set, which shuts the door on opportunities to learn from the wisdom of others who are able to help them achieve better results.

---

*People who refuse to receive instruction or correction are headed toward poverty.*

---

The fifth characteristic that leads to poverty is addictive behaviors and a lack of temperance (Proverbs 23:21). Destructive habits, such as drunkenness, gluttony, pornography, and anything else we allow to become an addiction, can lead to poverty. Spending money on or investing in the lust of the world rather than the kingdom of God is a wealth stealer and blocks the flow of blessings into our lives.

Poverty characteristic number six is following worthless people and pursuits. When this characteristic is present, it can certainly lead to lack and financial poverty. Proverbs 28:19 says, *"He who cultivates his land will have plenty of bread, but he who follows worthless people and pursuits will have poverty enough."* We shouldn't be so quick to fall for get-rich-quick business opportunities and people who make lavish promises of wealth. Again, we need to hear from God about what we choose to invest in. Godly wisdom will save us every time.

The seventh characteristic of poverty is hastening to be rich only for selfish reasons. Proverbs 28:22 states: *"He who has an evil and covetous eye hastens to be rich and knows not that want will come upon him."* When we are willing to do *anything* to be rich, at any cost, even if it means damaging people's lives or compromising our character and what we know to be true from God's Word, we are operating with a poverty mentality.

## Breaking a Poverty Mentality

There are many things that can indicate that a person has a poverty mentality. I touch on seven key areas in which you can examine your thinking to determine if change is necessary. Locating where you are is the first step toward breaking free.

### 1. You Find Excuses for the Lack in Your Life Instead of Dealing with the Root Issue

Making excuses or blaming others for your situation is a clear indication that you have a poverty mentality. The Bible says that a causeless curse doesn't come. In other words, there is a reason why you are in the situation you are in. However, if you don't discover the root cause and instead continue to complain, make excuses, and refuse godly instruction, you will stay where you are.

### 2. You are Critical of Those Who Teach and Preach Prosperity

Many people criticize preachers who teach from the Word of God about prosperity. Therefore, many ministers are afraid to teach about prosperity because they fear what people will think and say. But God wants the good news to get out. He wants to prosper His people! The Bible contains more Scriptures on wealth and prosperity than it does on heaven. When you are critical of those who teach the Word on prosperity, it shows that you have taken on the ideas and concepts of society. According to the world, when a preacher gives a sermon on prosperity, he is trying to get money. While there are some corrupt preachers, there are also those who are called to preach God's Word about prosperity.

*The Bible contains more Scriptures on wealth and*
*prosperity than it does on heaven.*

## 3. You Hate to See a Man or Woman of God Prosper

One of the best ways to receive God's provision is to sow into the lives of those who have worked the principles and are seeing results. We shouldn't be okay with seeing evil people prosper while hating to see a man or woman of God prosper. We all can succeed in God's kingdom; however, we cannot succeed if we are envious and jealous of another person's progress. We must deal with envy and jealousy by asking God to give us the grace to see things His way. We can ask Him to help us to rejoice with those who are blessed. Then we can expect to see His blessing manifest in our lives as well.

## 4. You Ask, "Is It Really Necessary to Tithe and Give Offerings?"

Sowing financially into the kingdom of God through tithes and offerings is God's system of operation for financial increase. However, God wants us to bring our tithes and offerings with a willing and loving heart. He wants us to bring our tithes and offerings as an act of love and appreciation toward Him, not because of a law. When we honor His Word concerning our giving, we will receive His blessing upon our finances (Proverbs 3:9). Honor and love go hand in hand.

## 5. You Are Afraid to Give Your Finances Under the Direction of the Holy Spirit and the Written Word of God

Poverty is indeed a mind-set that is governed by the fear of not having enough. People with a poverty mind-set are stingy and afraid to release money. They are often grieved when God speaks to them about sowing finances into the life of another person.

I know people who have money but still have a poverty mentality. A poverty mentality will put us in a position where we limit prosperity to only money. While that money (we're holding on to) may be available today, it may be gone tomorrow. Why? Because we must understand how God's system of increase operates. We cannot have a poverty mentality and expect to have His kind of increase.

> *We cannot have a poverty mentality and expect to have His kind of increase.*

Anytime fear is present in our lives, selfishness, which is the opposite of love, is present also. God is love, so we cannot separate Him from love. Fear is a sure way to remain in lack and poverty. If we are afraid to sow financially under the leading of the Holy Spirit and in accordance with Scripture, it is an indication that we have a poverty mentality.

## 6. You Do Not Trust in God to Be Your Source

Remember, your job, business, and paychecks are not your sources of increase. God must be your only source. If not, you will fall apart when other avenues of financial provision fail you.

Don't depend on anyone or anything other than God to meet your needs. Have faith He will take care of you, as He has promised in His Word.

## 7. You Are Suspicious, Insecure, and Fearful of Those around You

There's that ugly word again: *fear*. Fear is the number one hindrance to your breakthrough. If you are suspicious of others, fearing that people will take your money, you do not have a revelation of God's love for you. Have more faith in having more than enough instead of having fear about not having enough. The resources of heaven abound with all you need and desire. Therefore, begin to meditate on your covenant with God and His love toward you so that you can get the spirit of fear out of your life (and finances) forever.

# Life Application

Ask the Holy Spirit to reveal to you any poverty-based beliefs you may have. Ask Him to help you get rid of them. Write down what He says concerning the root issues in your life regarding finances.

_____

_____

_____

_____

_____

_____

_____

_____

_____

# 7

# GOD'S WAY VERSUS THE WORLD'S WAY

There is a way which seems right to a man *and* appears straight before him, but at the end of it is the way of death.

—PROVERBS 14:12

Let the wicked forsake his way and the unrighteous man his thoughts; and let him return to the Lord, and He will have love, pity, *and* mercy for him, and to our God, for He will multiply to him His abundant pardon.

—ISAIAH 55:7

But seek (aim at and strive after) first of all His kingdom and His righteousness (His way of doing and being right), and then all these things taken together will be given you besides.

—MATTHEW 6:33

Jesus said to him, I am the Way and the Truth and the Life; no one comes to the Father except by (through) Me.

—JOHN 14:6

Almost everything in this world's system is based on the quick-fix method. Think of the advertisements you hear and see almost daily. For example, "Lose 30 pounds in 30 days!" or "Consolidate your bills today!" or "Get Your Instant Payday Loan!" In this age of endless social networks, limitless phone service, microwave ovens, supersonic travel, and e-mail, it seems nearly impossible for us to wait patiently for things to happen, especially when it concerns our finances.

Continuous overspending leads to debt accumulation. Running up charges on our credit cards due to reckless spending leads only to a harvest of insufficiency. But when we are good stewards of our money, we promote increase and abundance in our lives.

---

*Continuous overspending leads to*
*debt accumulation.*

---

Realistically, our best choice is to turn to the Word of God for the solution to our financial problems. Second Samuel 22:31 states: "As for God, his way is perfect; the word of the Lord is tried." In other words, the Word of God works! But it's up to us to apply those principles to our situations and circumstances.

Please know that I don't want anyone to feel condemned about overspending and accumulating debt. I've been there, too. However, since I've discovered God's Word and His principles for living, I completely trust the Holy Spirit's guidance. I receive His guidance through the written Word and the revelation knowledge He gives me. I know He will do the same for anyone who will submit to His leadership. Remember, it is by grace through faith that we have successful accomplishments in God's kingdom. I believe it is worth repeating that even with His Word and His principles we still must cultivate our relationship with Jesus Christ in order to receive wisdom concerning our specific situations.

## Two Systems Operating Simultaneously

Throughout the New Testament, Jesus frequently spoke of the *kingdom of God*. He was referring to one of two systems through which we can operate. When we break down the word *kingdom*, the prefix *king-* refers to a person or figure, while the suffix *-dom* refers to dominion, or sphere of influence. In other words, *kingdom* refers to an individual's realm of jurisdiction. Therefore, the kingdom of God is the manner in which God operates, or God's way of doing things. The same thing can be said of the words *world* and *worldly*—both refer to a method or standard of operation. For example, when we say someone is "worldly," we're saying they are living according to what society considers an acceptable standard of living. When we consider these definitions in the context of managing our finances, we're faced with a choice—either to handle our finances God's way or the world's way.

**Kingdom** *refers to an individual's realm of jurisdiction.*

While the world's system promotes the idea of piling on debt and living beyond our means, it also has a system for getting rid of debt. Most of us have already tried to get out of debt through the world's system of bill consolidation, second mortgages, credit counseling, and bankruptcy. However, none of these methods permanently resolve the problem because they foster dependency. Think about it. You borrow money only to have to borrow more to pay for the money you already owe! And on top of owing money to the lending company, you have to pay interest, too!

For example, if you purchase an item with your credit card and make the monthly payment on time, every time—guess what? Your credit limit increases. The more you buy, the more you're able to buy. But, again, you have to pay interest, which means that you're actually paying *more* for the item than you would have if you had simply waited to buy it with cash! It just doesn't make sense. Whether you want to admit it or not, the world's system promotes debt. In addition, it teaches you to put away money while you're young so that you can become wealthy when you are old. Although that *sounds* reasonable, and I certainly believe in saving money, I think most of us would prefer to be millionaires at thirty, forty, fifty, and sixty. No matter how we look at it, the world's system is just another tactic of the enemy to keep us in financial bondage.

The Bible refers to Satan as the ruler of this present world (John 12:31; 16:11). In other words, the world's system, or its way of doing things, belongs to him. However, Believers can participate in God's system, which promotes prosperity, peace, and the Gospel message. Jesus said, *"My kingdom is not of this world"* (John 18:36), which means that God's system goes completely against the status quo.

## The Better Way

God's system works through something called seedtime and harvest. Let me explain. Do you remember the golden rule: "Do unto others as you would have them do unto you"? This statement actually refers to the principle of sowing and reaping found in Galatians 6:7—"For whatsoever a man soweth, that shall he also reap" (KJV). Simply put, whatever you do to or for others will come back to you, whether it's good or bad.

---

*God's system works through something called seedtime and harvest.*

---

This same rule can also be applied to finances. God's system is based on giving and receiving. It sounds like a bad way of dealing with our finances, doesn't it? But remember, God's system is the exact opposite of the world's system. It is the better way. The world tells us to hoard every penny we have, while God's system tells us to give in order to receive. However, the key to seeing positive results is obedience to God in our giving. I call Matthew 13:3 the grandfather parable of them all. If we can get a good understanding of this Scripture, we will most likely understand just about everything else in the Bible. Matthew 13:3 says: *"Behold, a sower went forth to sow"* (KJV). A farmer *has* to sow if he wants a harvest. And just as the farmer will never harvest a crop by hoarding his seed, neither will we get out of debt by hoarding our money.

In Luke 6:38, Jesus tells us to *"give and it shall be given unto you; good measure, pressed down, and shaken together, and running over, shall men give into your bosom."* Notice the first thing we are told to do: "*Give*, and it shall be given unto you." When we give to others, it opens the door for people to give to us. Whatever we give will be returned. Unfortunately, this mind-set is a problem for many Christians. They think it's okay to give every now and then, but to give all the time? No way! It's one thing to say, "I want to be out of debt and financially successful," but it's something entirely different to become disciplined enough to actually get there. I believe the way in which we handle our finances pretty much determines how we handle everything else in life.

This includes how we handle our paychecks. Our paychecks are not to be used as a means through which to get out of debt because our paychecks won't be enough to take care of our households and everything God tells us to do. Our jobs are merely avenues through which we can collect financial and material seed. We work in order to get financial seed to plant into good ground (in someone's life or ministry). In the same way that a farmer lives off of the harvest of his crop, so we, too, should live off the harvest of the seeds we have sown.

---

*Our jobs are merely avenues through which we can collect financial and material seed.*

---

Consider the call of God on my life. I could make millions of dollars a year, and it still wouldn't be enough to pay for the television programming needed to reach the millions of people who have not yet heard the Gospel for the first time, or those who need to be discipled on a daily basis. Therefore, it is vital that we begin to see money as a means to an end. In other words, money is a tool God can use to further the Gospel. I am living proof that the way out of debt is through giving. We must develop a mind-set to give to live, and then live to give.

## Learning to Give

Learning to give is fundamental to Christianity. Our willingness to give to others is the measuring stick of our spiritual maturity. That's a tough pill to swallow, considering that most Christians treat giving as a grievous obligation rather than as a joy. In 2 Corinthians 9:7, Paul states that *"God loveth a cheerful giver"* (KJV). In other words, there is no real benefit in reluctant giving. It makes God feel as though we really don't want anything to do with His plans and purposes. And, believe it or not, when we give grudgingly, that is exactly what we are doing—resenting God's ultimate plan, which is to fund the message of the Gospel. When we give reluctantly, we experience a sense of loss; however, giving should not be seen as loss but as gain. Sowing allows us to release something in order to get a hundredfold return on what we have sown. And there are few investments, if any, that yield a hundredfold return.

---

*When we give reluctantly, we experience
a sense of loss; however, giving should not be
seen as loss but as gain.*

---

Before you give, you should remember to:

### 1. Renew Your Mind

Without renewing your mind with the Word of God regarding giving, you won't have the faith to give. When you sow financial seed with the knowledge of God's Word, you will know beyond a shadow of a doubt that your seed will bring a hundredfold return.

## 2. Sow into Good Ground

The Word of God assures you in Luke 8:5–8 that abundance is on the way when you sow in *good* ground. Some examples of good ground include certain ministries, special projects, the lives of other Believers, and the life of your man or woman of God. It is important to sow only where the Holy Spirit leads you to do so. He's the only One who knows what is inside a person's heart. In 1 Samuel 16:7, He told the prophet Samuel, *"The Lord seeth not as man seeth; for man looketh on the outward appearance, but the Lord looketh on the heart"* (KJV). Don't be deceived by outward appearances. Trust the Holy Spirit for direction and allow Him to guide your giving. Your obedience will yield a tremendous harvest.

## 3. Give in Faith, Knowing You Will Receive

Jesus stated in Luke 6:38 that when you give, it will be given back to you. For example, the human body can exhale only for a certain amount of time before it signals a need for oxygen. At that point, the body inhales, rejuvenating the system. It's a cycle instituted by God: inhale, exhale, inhale, exhale. We will die if we do only one or the other. The same is true in the area of giving and receiving. We don't do one or the other; we must do both. Therefore, whenever you give by faith, expect to receive.

## 4. Remember that a Seed Grows Down Before It Grows Up

The Bible tells us in Mark 4:26–27 that the kingdom of God is *"as if a man should cast seed into the ground; And should sleep, and rise night and day, and the seed should spring and grow up, he knoweth not how"* (KJV). In other words, allow time for your seed to grow and develop. Don't put it in the ground and then stand over it. Your harvest will come only after the root has grown deep into the ground of your heart. By planting the Word of God in your heart, saying your faith Scriptures aloud several times a day, and acting on your faith, you will see results.

---

*Your harvest will come only after the root has*
*grown deep into the ground of your heart.*

---

## 5. Help Someone Who Has a Similar Need

If you want God to release you from your debt, sow the seed of debt release into someone else's life. The same force you exert to help someone else get out of debt opens the door for God to get you out of debt. *"For with the same measure that ye mete withal it shall be measured to you again"* (Luke 6:38 KJV). In other words, do for someone else first what you would like to have done for you. If you want to buy a car debt free, contribute toward someone else's efforts to buy a car debt free. If you want a loan cancelled, help someone else pay off his or her loan.

You're probably thinking, *Brother Dollar, if I could do that, my debt would be paid off by now!* I'm not asking you to pay off the entire debt. I am, however, encouraging you to give what God tells you to give toward the debt amount.

Make a quality decision to divorce yourself from the world's system and, instead, begin to employ God's method of sowing and reaping. God has a perfect plan to get you out of debt and into financial freedom, but if you continue to run back to your former way of doing things, you'll never get anywhere. Matthew

6:33 commands us to *"seek (aim at and strive after) first of all His kingdom and His righteousness (His way of doing and being right),"* so that God may grant us the things we desire.

---

*Make a quality decision to divorce yourself from the world's system and, instead, begin to employ God's method of sowing and reaping.*

---

# Life Application

Ask the Holy Spirit to give you more insight and revelation on God's way of doing things, and show specific ways in which you can free up finances or add income to your household so that you can give and live financially free. Write down His instructions.

_____

_____

_____

_____

_____

_____

_____

_____

_____

_____

_____

_____

# GRACE FOR LIVING SUCCESSFULLY

8

For out of His fullness (abundance) we have all received [all had a share and we were all supplied with] one grace after another *and* spiritual blessing upon spiritual blessing *and* even favor upon favor *and* gift [heaped] upon gift.
For while the Law was given through Moses, grace (unearned, undeserved favor and spiritual blessing) and truth came through Jesus Christ.

—JOHN 1:16–17

Let us then fearlessly *and* confidently *and* boldly draw near to the throne of grace (the throne of God's unmerited favor to us sinners), that we may receive mercy [for our failures] and find grace to help in good time for every need [appropriate help and well-timed help, coming just when we need it].

—HEBREWS 4:16

In the first half of this book, I focused on knowing God and hearing His voice. In the second half, I will focus on God's grace for living and the power of wisdom from His Word. You have probably heard the term "God's grace" used before, and perhaps you've heard it defined as "God's unmerited favor." While the favor and love of God are aspects of His grace, it is much more than this. God's grace is His supernatural power, which enables us to overcome our shortcomings and serve Him acceptably.

God didn't just give us grace (His empowerment) to deliver us from our sin; He also gave us grace to live successfully on this earth. Many Christians do not understand how to tap into the power that God has placed in them. The same grace we received to become born again is the same grace we receive to live victoriously. Through faith, we can obtain the grace to do anything we need to do, including discovering God's will for our lives.

---

*God didn't just give us grace (His empowerment) to deliver us from our sin; He also gave us grace to live successfully on this earth.*

---

When Jesus came to the earth, He taught about grace and truth. He gave us the whole truth about the grace of God (John 1:16–17).

God's grace is not some vague religious concept. It is His divine power. We have everything we need to live a life that pleases Him (2 Peter 1:3) because He placed His grace within our born-again spirits. It is this grace that empowers us as Believers, not our own human efforts alone.

We cannot work to obtain God's grace. There is nothing we have done to earn salvation, which means there is nothing we can do to earn God's grace. All we have to do is receive it by faith. Once we have a revelation of God's grace, we can depend on it as we carry out our daily activities. Whether we are faced with choosing the right place to live, the right career, or managing our finances God's way, we must know how to follow our peace and depend on God's grace when making decisions in life.

However, while we are depending on God's grace, we know that there are some practical things we have to do to live in this natural world. When we are waiting to receive a rhema Word from God concerning an issue we're facing, we have to continue to make other decisions as we work, pay our bills, raise our families, and manage our finances. As we perform our day-to-day activities, we need to know how to operate in godly wisdom in every area of our lives.

When we choose to make the Word our final authority, we tap into the wisdom of God. I like the way my wife, Taffi, defines wisdom. She says it is getting the knowledge and understanding of how to proceed when we don't know what to do. For example, many Christians who are unemployed think they can simply sit and wait to receive a Word from God without making any effort to look for a job. Someone who doesn't have a job should get up every morning to look for one while depending on God's grace to succeed. The Word doesn't support laziness. God doesn't usually tell us to do the things we already know to do. He tells us what we don't know.

*God doesn't usually tell us to do the things we
already know to do. He tells us what we don't know.*

## Allow Grace to Abound in Your Finances

Many times we struggle to fix what is wrong in our lives, often elim-
inating God in the process. Our own efforts usually leave us frustrated and fruitless. Depending on His grace is a more effective way
to live. It strengthens our relationship with God because we are inviting Him to be involved in our decisions. In other words, we rely on
His Word and His counsel to succeed in life. We acknowledge Him as
our primary source, not just one of our resources. Furthermore, we
require God's grace to meet our needs on a daily basis. Second Corinthians 9:8 says: *"God is able to make all grace (every favor and earthly
blessing) come to you in abundance, so that you may always and under all
circumstances and whatever the need be self-sufficient [possessing enough to
require no aid or support and furnished in abundance for every good work
and charitable donation]."* According to this Scripture, it is through the
grace of God that we always have all sufficiency in all things, and
increase in every good work. The only thing required to access God's
grace is faith, which comes by hearing the Word of God.

For example, when I became a born-again Christian, it was in
response to hearing the Word of God preached about salvation.
Then I made a decision to turn from my sins. I confessed with my
mouth and believed in my heart that Jesus died and rose for me,
and I asked Him to come into my life. I received my salvation by
grace through faith. The same manner in which we received our
salvation is the same way we will receive everything else we need
in the kingdom of God—by grace through faith (Ephesians 2:8–9).

When we understand and meditate on the Word concerning financial provision, we position ourselves to receive revelation from God. One way of meditating on the Word is by speaking the Word. When we hear ourselves repeat the Word of God, we stir up our faith. Once our faith is stirred up, we will begin to receive the wisdom we need to increase financially. Additionally, this process will work for every area of our lives. In this way, we are ultimately empowered by Him to gain financial provision. We should stir up our faith and expectation to receive His grace every day.

*When we understand and meditate on the Word concerning financial provision, we position ourselves to receive revelation from God.*

## Grace to Do the Works of God

God created you for a good purpose, and that purpose is designed to bring Him pleasure and glory. Every gift, talent, and ability God has given us is for the specific purpose of ultimately glorifying Him. The paths that He has planned for us are good paths that lead to abundance. The grace of God on our lives gives us the ability to do everything He has called us to do as we allow our steps to be ordered by Him.

Revelation 4:11 says, *"Thou art worthy, O Lord, to receive glory and honor and power: for thou hast created all things, and for thy pleasure they are and were created"* (KJV). God has created us to do good works, and the works of God that we are ordained to carry out can be done only through our relationship with Jesus Christ. The grace of God is the catalyst that enables us to do great things for the kingdom of God.

God will never let us compete with His grace. When we try to do things in our own way, we are actually operating in pride because we are essentially saying that our way is better than God's way. Even as it relates to changing certain bad habits we have, we must understand that willpower is not the answer. God has empowered us to overcome our flesh through His grace so we don't have to rely on ourselves to get the job done.

---

*God will never let us compete with His grace.*

---

There may be something you are feeling led to do that is going to require the grace of God. He may have given you an idea or a concept that is going to impact many lives. Remember that grace and faith are connected, and faith comes from the Word of God. When you find out what the Bible says about the issues you face, or you receive a spoken Word from God that confirms what you are setting out to do, the grace of God causes your endeavors to succeed.

Second Corinthians 12:9–10 says, *"And he said unto me, My grace is sufficient for thee: for my strength is made perfect in weakness. Most gladly therefore will I rather glory in my infirmities, that the power of Christ may rest upon me. Therefore I take pleasure in infirmities, in reproaches, in necessities, in persecutions, in distresses for Christ's sake: for when I am weak, then am I strong"* (KJV). Whenever you feel weak or incapable of carrying out what God has called you to do, even as it relates to obeying His Word, remember that the power of Christ is inside you, strengthening you. His strength is the grace you need to be successful. It doesn't matter if all of hell comes against you; God's grace is sufficient. Act on your faith by doing a corresponding action in line with what you believe, and grace will put you over the top. Get yourself out of the way so God's power can work in you and through you to do what He has called you to do.

# Life Application

In chapter 5 of this book, I provided you with a list of declarations you can speak over your finances and debt. Here are some declarations on grace that will help you to continue to decree that God is able to make all grace increase toward you and that you always, under all circumstances, have whatever you need to be self-sufficient! Confess that you have abundant life by grace through faith! I believe if you stay in faith by confessing the Word and hearing the Word, your faith will be ignited, and your lack will begin to disappear.

### Grace Declarations

*By grace through faith, I believe I have received the ability to hear God's voice and receive the knowledge of His specific will for my life for this day.*

*I release my faith for the grace to live a life that pleases God. I am able to serve Him acceptably through grace.*

*Through grace, I have the ability to obey God's Word. I am no longer a slave to sin, nor am I subject to it.*

*I walk by faith and not by what my physical senses tell me.*

*I can do all things through Christ who strengthens me. His grace makes me an overcomer. Through grace I know God's perfect will for my life.*

*Grace is not earned; it is received by faith. I receive the benefits of God's grace in my life through faith in His Word.*

*Jesus Christ, who is the manifested Word of God, is the only channel of grace. I have the full nature of Christ within me, and I partake of that nature through the Word.*

*God is able to make all grace (every favor and earthly blessing) increase in my life. I have a grace to cover every area of my life.*

*I possess a grace for giving.*

*I possess a grace for overcoming anger, lust, and all other evil emotions that lead to sin.*

*I am empowered to prosper and have success in every area of my life through God's grace. I withdraw grace from my re-created spirit by renewing my mind with the Word.*

*I acknowledge all the supernatural resources I have within my spirit, and I use my faith to transfer those resources into the physical realm.*

*I release the grace of God through praying in tongues. I renew my strength through my personal prayer language, and I make spiritual progress.*

*I walk in the fear of the Lord by respecting and honoring Him in all that I do.*

*Through grace, I am able to walk in true holiness and godliness. I overcome any and all bondage through the supernatural empowerment of God.*

# MAKING WISE DECISIONS

9

Who is the man who reverently fears *and* worships
the Lord? Him shall He teach in the way that he
should choose.

—PSALM 25:12

For this world's wisdom is foolishness (absurdity
and stupidity) with God, for it is written, He lays
hold of the wise in their [own] craftiness...

—1 CORINTHIANS 3:19

I have strength for all things in Christ Who
empowers me [I am ready for anything and equal
to anything through Him Who infuses inner
strength into me; I am self-sufficient in Christ's
sufficiency].

—PHILIPPIANS 4:13

In this way laying up for themselves
[the riches that endure forever as] a good
foundation for the future, so that they may
grasp that which is life indeed.

—1 TIMOTHY 6:19

When I was a young child, my family did not have much financially. I remember making a decision to do whatever I could to bring my family out of lack and poverty. That decision opened the door to what my life is today. Many people look at the success and wealth I've acquired and totally disregard the hard work, discipline, and diligence it took to obtain it. They don't understand that I had to make some hard decisions. But those decisions were based on the Word of God and lifted me from one position to the next. I had to gain more and more knowledge every step of the way.

In Deuteronomy 30:19, God tells us that He made us free moral agents, and that we have the right to choose between life or death, a blessing or a curse. Life constantly offers us opportunities to make decisions on a daily basis. When the alarm goes off in the morning, we decide whether to get out of bed or sleep in. When we receive money, we decide whether to spend it on things we want or the things we need. Our decisions determine the quality of our lives.

*Our decisions determine the quality of our lives.*

Every decision is an open door to reality. Once we make a choice, we have opened the door to a particular outcome. For example, if you are not prospering financially, it's not that God hasn't given you what you need to gain wealth. It may be because you have not acquired the practical knowledge needed to become successful in that area. Your financial decisions have been based on the information you've acquired throughout your life. However, bad information leads to bad decisions. The question we should ask ourselves is, *What information have I based my major decisions on?*

The people we have had relationships with throughout the years have impacted our lives in major ways. This is why we should be cautious about what and whom we allow to influence us. Family members are a major source of information for most people, but loved ones may not be the best source of information. We can determine whether to take a person's advice by looking at his or her life and observing whether he or she has made wise decisions. We may have grown up with a certain mind-set that developed from the impartations of family and close friends; however, we should consider the habits we've formed and discard the ones that do not line up with the Word. These habits may be hard to break at first, but we can do all things through Christ (Philippians 4:13).

God's Word is the wisdom we need to govern our lives, and whatever contradicts it will lead us down the wrong path. We can find information that opposes the Word in many media outlets, from TV talk shows, reality shows, and radio talk shows to magazines and books. The producers of a majority of this information seek only to affirm society's norms and values. The problem is their ideals are so popular that they appear to be normal to most Christians. But if it doesn't line up with the Word, it cannot be accepted. The Word of God has to be the foundation for our lives. When we choose the world's way of doing things over God's, we should not be surprised when things don't work out the way we want them to.

> *The Word of God has to be the foundation*
> *for our lives.*

The Bible is God's instruction manual for life. It is more than a decorative piece for the coffee table. We must open His Word and study it if we want to make wise decisions. The Word of God will not get into our brains by osmosis. Unless we tap into God's wisdom, we will do things out of our own belief system or knowledge base that we've developed over time, which will be limited, and in some cases flat-out wrong.

Obtaining the right information is critical to our ability to make sound decisions. When we choose to make the Word our final authority, we begin to display wisdom in all our decisions. As I stated previously, wisdom is having knowledge and understanding about how to proceed when we don't know what to do.

Making wise decisions is about knowing how to use the knowledge we have in any given situation. For instance, although my mother knew how to prepare a full-course meal, it was wisdom that enabled her to prepare a meal for the whole family with only a few items in the refrigerator or cupboard. We have wisdom when we know how to apply our knowledge to achieve a proper outcome.

> *Making wise decisions is about knowing how to use*
> *the knowledge we have in any given situation.*

I know you're probably saying, *Okay, I get it, there's a difference between knowledge and wisdom; but how do I get the wisdom to make the right decisions?* James 1:5 says, *"If any of you lack wisdom, let him ask of God, that giveth to all men liberally, and upbraideth not; and it shall be given him"* (KJV). If you need wisdom, simply ask for it! When you do, God imparts His insight into you for your specific situation. Asking God for wisdom is one way of acknowledging Him in all your ways. It is essentially saying, "Lord, I don't know what to do. I need your help."

Our lives are comprised of a series of choices. Where we end up is a result of the decisions we have made. We cannot blame the devil or anyone else for where we are. Many people take on the victim role and feel more comfortable blaming others for their lots in life, but at some point they will have to take responsibility. God has made us free moral agents and will never violate our right to choose. In Deuteronomy 30:19, God explains in more detail the free will He has given us. The Scripture says, "I call Heaven and Earth to witness against you today: I place before you Life and Death, Blessing and Curse. Choose life so that you and your children will live" (MSG). God loves us so much. His desire is that we would choose His way. However, He will not make that decision for us. Neither can Satan force us to choose *his* way. Both God and Satan only present us with choices and leave the decisions to us.

## Setting Boundaries

We must be honest with ourselves in order to make a quality decision. Growth can't occur until we acknowledge that we need to change. I can always tell how serious a person is about a decision based on the boundaries he or she has established. For example, a person may *want* to lose weight, but it will never come to pass if he or she does not set boundaries. For instance, if a person has a weakness for doughnuts, he or she will avoid going near the doughnut shop. Boundaries are put in place to protect our decisions. When boundaries are established, and we commit to maintaining them, our desires become realities.

---

*I can always tell how serious a person is
about a decision based on the boundaries he
or she has established.*

---

The same is true when we make a decision to choose God's way. We must then decide to protect that decision by placing boundaries around it. We can no longer entertain people and sources of information that contradict God's Word. When the enemy brings suggestions to our minds, we must learn how to cast them down by speaking the Scriptures concerning the situation. However, if we don't place boundaries around our decision to follow the Word, we can easily get sidetracked or distracted by the things going on in this world.

## Foolish Decisions Are Costly

A blessing comes as a result of making godly decisions. A curse is an empowerment to fail, and failure comes as a result of foolish decisions. Foolish decisions are decisions that are not in line with the Word of God, and they are quite expensive. For example, a married man who decides to commit adultery will have to deal with many costly outcomes as a result of his foolish decision. Unwanted pregnancy, disease, and divorce are just a few. Besides that, the emotional and spiritual damage that can occur as a result of his infidelity only adds fuel to the fire. His decision to sin will cost him money, time, energy, and, most important, his peace of mind.

---

*A blessing comes as a result of making godly decisions.*

---

As we mentioned in previous chapters, God's grace empowers us to do what we cannot do with our own abilities. When we choose to operate in wisdom, we can trust God's grace to give us the advantage. Additionally, the Holy Spirit is always there to direct us into victory. Please be reminded that following God's Word and the leadership of the Holy Spirit is a process. We cannot beat ourselves up when things go wrong, nor can we ignore mistakes. However, when we make a mistake, we can always turn to the Holy Spirit and ask Him to help us follow His guidance. We don't have to go through life not knowing what to do or how to handle situations we face. By operating in God's wisdom, we can be successful and avoid the enemy's traps. I encourage you to yield to the Holy Spirit and obey God's Word so that every decision you make will be a godly one.

# Life Application

From this day forward, whenever you are faced with a decision, ask God for wisdom. And during your prayer time, ask Him to give you more revelation on how to make wise decisions. Then write down what you believe He is speaking to your heart.

# CHOOSING THE RIGHT CAREER
# (YOUR GOD-GIVEN ASSIGNMENT)

10

For God's gifts and His call are irrevocable.
[He never withdraws them when once they are
given, and He does not change His mind about
those to whom He gives His grace or to whom
He sends His call.]

—ROMANS 11:29

And there are distinctive varieties of operation
[of working to accomplish things], but it is
the same God Who inspires *and* energizes
them all in all.

—1 CORINTHIANS 12:6

Because of this, brethren, be all the more
solicitous *and* eager to make sure (to ratify,
to strengthen, to make steadfast) your calling
and election; for if you do this, you will never
stumble *or* fall.

—2 PETER 1:10

[For it is He] Who delivered *and* saved us
and called us with a calling in itself holy *and*
leading to holiness [to a life of consecration,
a vocation of holiness]...

—2 TIMOTHY 1:9A

Choosing the right career should not be treated as a trivial matter. I often hear people say, "As long as I am working and getting paid, that's all that matters." However, our career choices can affect every area of our lives, including our marriages and families, and they also affect our service to God. In today's society, the job market is always changing. Therefore, it is important to avoid making wrong career choices, which could lead to a lack of passion and purpose, and even financial hardship. Additionally, since the job market is always changing, making the wrong career choice could lead to financial hardship.

Many times we make career choices without first discovering God's purpose for our lives. That was exactly what I did while I was in college. I had my own plans for my life. I began to pursue them, and then somewhere along the way I asked God to bless my efforts. But that is not how it works. We don't get to *choose* the path God has set for our lives; we *discover* it by seeking Him for direction before we pursue our own plan. No matter what career we choose, we will find true success only in what God has called us to do. True success is discovering and fulfilling the will of God for our lives.

*No matter what career we choose, we will find true*
*success only in what God has called us to do.*

## True Success

Have you ever seen people who look successful by the world's standards, yet they still seem incomplete or broken somehow? We see it every day in the media. People achieve fame and fortune, yet at the end of their lives it is obvious that they didn't find true success, because fame and wealth did not give them fulfillment in their personal lives.

Proverbs 10:22 says, *"The blessing of the Lord, it makes [truly] rich, and He adds no sorrow with it, [neither does toiling increase it]."* We can't allow ourselves to get seduced into a career just because it pays well or sounds impressive according to the world's standards. We should choose a career based on what we believe God wants us to do. As we follow His will for our lives and commit to trusting Him, He will lead us into wholeness, where there is nothing missing or broken in our lives.

I can remember when I believed with every fiber of my being that I was going to play professional football. I had it all mapped out. I planned my life according to what I envisioned for my future. I lifted weights, bench-pressed, and rigorously studied football playbooks. I had big dreams, but I never stopped to ask God what *He* wanted me to do. So, when my college football career abruptly ended due to an injury, I was at the lowest point in my life. That was when I finally humbled myself and began to seek God and His plan for my life. It was not until I was in His will that I began to see the manifestation of everything I desired in my life. I am convinced that even if I had succeeded as a pro football player, my life still would have been missing something. *True* success only comes when we are in the will of God.

## Asking God First

When it comes to choosing the right career, seeking God's wisdom and guidance must be our priority. So many people make the mistake of choosing careers solely on the basis of money. However, money should never be our main focus, because God knows all of our needs, and He will supply. When we get direction from Him, we will ultimately find the career path God has destined for us, along with His provision.

*When it comes to choosing the right career, seeking God's wisdom and guidance must be our priority.*

Matthew 6:33 says, *"But seek (aim at and strive after) first of all His kingdom and His righteousness (His way of doing and being right), and then all these things taken together will be given you besides."* His way of doing and being right also means showing Him respect and choosing a career that honors Him. When we honor God, His Word and His voice inside of us weigh heavier in our lives than anything else. Because we honor Him, we would not take a job that would cause us to compromise our integrity or go against the principles found in the Word of God. Acknowledging God is truly vital to choosing the right career path in life.

## The Practical Side

When we seek God and honor Him, we carry out the spiritual aspects that are required when choosing the right career. There are also some things we must do in the natural. Just as it is important to do what's needed in the spiritual realm, it is equally important to do what's needed in the natural.

Once we have prepared ourselves spiritually, here are eleven practical things we can consider when choosing a career:

## 1. Begin with Your Values

How important to you is this career you are considering? Does it compromise your values or the Word of God?

## 2. Are You Passionate about This Career?

Passion and service are two key elements to achieving success. Once you find something you would do for free, you have found your passion, which can lead you to great success in life.

## 3. Locate Your Skills and Talents

There is a distinction between skills and talents. Your skills are things you have been trained to do, while your talent is something you do naturally. Keep in mind that just because you've been trained to do something doesn't necessarily mean that you'll enjoy it. Your success is directly connected to discovering what you have been graced to do.

## 4. Identify Your Preferences

Consider what you enjoy doing and what you hate doing. Be honest with yourself when answering these questions. It is okay if you find you don't like certain careers. Start by making a list of careers you *do* like and a list of careers you *don't* like. This process will help you eliminate career choices you definitely don't want to make. You will never be successful doing something you don't want to do.

## 5. Become Broadly Literate

Try to learn as much as you can about the career you are considering. Gather as much information as possible, including the future of the industry or profession. Additionally, research the companies or organizations you want to work for.

## 6. Experiment

Through volunteer and apprenticeship programs, you can discover whether or not a job fits you and if it is something you will enjoy. In my opinion, this is a very wise move when considering a career. You will have a chance to experience the day-to-day operations within that field. Nothing takes the place of *valuable* experience. Ultimately, you will be able to confidently say, "Yes, I'm going in the right direction. This is a good career choice for me." Or, the experience may lead you to decide to reconsider your career choice, and that's fine, too. That's what experimentation is all about.

## 7. Opt for Experience First, Money Second

Take advantage of every opportunity to become the best at what you do. Ask yourself, "Which position will offer me the best chance of becoming excellent at what I do?"

## 8. Aim for a Job in Which You Can Give a 110 Percent Commitment

This is a very important part of your success. Today's job market has a low tolerance for people who don't put forth their best efforts. Employers are always looking to replace people who don't give their all on their jobs. They are looking for people who are enthusiastic and productive at all times. With the economy leveling, downsizing has become an acceptable and common practice. It's no wonder that modest to average performance won't cut it in today's job market.

## 9. Build Your Lifestyle around Your Actual Income, Not Your Expectation

No matter how much money you expect to make in the future, your financial and personal goals should fit what you actually make now. Do not live beyond your means because you are expecting a raise. Too often, people get into financial binds by planning and spending money they hope to make in the near future, and when that doesn't happen, they end up being in over their heads and stressed out.

## 10. Invest 5 Percent of Your Time, Energy, and Money in Furthering Your Career

Read books, surf the Internet, or take online courses that will allow you to further develop and grow in your field. Also, be sure to check with your employer for continuing education or career advancement classes. Today, many employers allow advance training programs at no cost to employees.

## 11. Be Willing to Change and Adapt

Be flexible. Don't be so rigid that you're not open to new opportunities and are unable to make necessary adjustments when God is trying to direct you. Be willing to allow God to lead you in the direction He has planned for you.

Be sure to allow the Holy Spirit to guide you as you proceed in doing the practical things concerning your career. If you don't feel something is the best choice for you, don't ignore that inner leading. The Holy Spirit will direct your steps if you allow Him to. He will lead you into the right career, one that is fulfilling and honorable.

---

*The Holy Spirit will direct your steps*
*if you allow Him to.*

---

Proverbs 3:5–6 says, "Lean on, trust in, and be confident in the Lord with all your heart and mind, and do not rely on your own insight or understanding. In all your ways know, recognize and acknowledge Him, and He will direct and make straight and plain your paths."

# Life Application

Begin praying daily about your career. What do you believe the Holy Spirit is saying to you in response? Write down and obey what the Holy Spirit tells you.

_____

_____

_____

_____

_____

_____

_____

_____

_____

_____

# GOOD WORK ETHICS

11

He becomes poor who works with a slack *and* idle hand, but the hand of the diligent makes rich.

—PROVERBS 10:4


So I saw that there is nothing better than that a man should rejoice in his own works, for that is his portion. For who shall bring him back to see what will happen after he is gone?

—ECCLESIASTES 3:22


And whatever you do [no matter what it is] in word or deed, do everything in the name of the Lord Jesus *and* in [dependence upon] His Person, giving praise to God the Father through Him.

—COLOSSIANS 3:17

In previous chapters, I have shared how the Holy Spirit helps us with the issues we face every day. He even pays attention to our attitudes toward our jobs. Our jobs (whether operating a business or working for a company) are our God-given assignments. Therefore, our attitudes regarding the work we do and how we carry out each detail are crucial to achieving success God's way.

Many people become complacent in their jobs, particularly if they have worked for an employer for a long period of time. That lackadaisical approach hurts them because their attitude and the quality of their work determine their overall success. Good work ethics add value to employees. How we perform our assigned tasks is just as important as choosing the right job or business. Fortunately, some of us were fortunate enough to be raised by parents who instilled strong work ethics and values in us, but not everyone had that experience. As a result, many people lack good work ethics because they simply were not taught how to develop them.

*How we perform our assigned tasks is just as important as choosing the right job or business.*

Good work ethics are basically codes of conduct that are followed on the job. They are an issue of character, which is doing what is right because it's right. Arriving to work on time, performing your assignments in excellence, having respect for those in authority, and using the time at work wisely are all good work ethics. When we display this level of character at work, we stand out from the crowd. People who have good work ethics are noticed by their employers and are often promoted based on their work ethics alone.

## Christians Work for God

It does not matter what our occupation may be, at the end of the day we must establish within our minds that we are actually working for God. When we work with this mind-set, we will most likely do our jobs well because we want to please Him. We will find ourselves doing what is right all of the time instead of only when we think someone is watching. The Bible gives practical wisdom for every area of life, including the area of work. Ephesians 6:5–7 (KJV) gives practical advice on how we should work:

> *Servants, be obedient to them that are your masters according to the flesh, with fear and trembling, in singleness of your heart, as unto Christ; Not with eyeservice, as menpleasers; but as the servants of Christ, doing the will of God from the heart; With good will doing service, as to the Lord, and not to men.*

*It does not matter what our occupation may be, at the end of the day we must establish within our minds that we are actually working for God.*

These Scriptures make it clear that we must not pretend to do our job well simply because others are watching. God looks at our hearts, and He knows the real deal. For example, a child who is told by his parent to sit down and be quiet may appear to be obedient when he takes his seat. But if the child has a bad attitude and flops down in the seat defiantly, he is still standing on the inside. Likewise, many adults hold an inner attitude of rebellion at work, which does not bring honor to God.

---

**God looks at our hearts, and He knows the real deal.**

---

Many years ago, I was given a job at the church I attended. My job was to clean the church. Although the job didn't pay well, I carried out my tasks in excellence. I made sure people were impressed when they entered the bathrooms. I took my time, attending to every detail as I cleaned. You may be thinking, *Well, what's so special about that?* I believe that God considered my heart while I was doing that job, and as a result He began to lead and guide me to the best path for my life.

We must be God-conscious at all times. Only then will we know what it means to work for God and not man. As we focus on doing a good job for Him, we stay on task and greatly improve the quality of our job performance.

Colossians 3:23 says, *"And whatsoever ye do, do it heartily, as to the Lord, and not unto men"* (KJV). When we become mindful of the fact that God's eyes are always on us, that He pays close attention to our every move, most of us will think twice about wasting time, loafing, or disrespecting others.

The person who works for God is concerned about how He views his or her performance. Moreover, when we strive to please God in all we do, others will be pleased with our work as well. As

Christians, we have the blessing on our lives, and it will spill over into our assignments at work. We are empowered to excel at whatever we have been assigned to do, and we can do it in excellence.

## Dress Your Mind for Work

It is necessary to prepare our minds before starting any job or task. Attitude is very important. Adjusting our attitudes *before* we get to the workplace positions us and those we encounter to have a good day. Often we do not realize it, but the way we carry ourselves at work helps create either a positive environment or a negative one. Our attitudes derive from our inner thoughts and self-talk. That is why we should judge ourselves in this area. We need to ask ourselves each day, *Am I a complainer? Do I have negative things to say about my work environment and coworkers? Do I contribute to making my workplace positive, or am I helping to make it negative?*

*Our attitudes derive from our inner thoughts and self-talk.*

Some of you may be thinking, *"Well, Brother Dollar, if you knew what I had to go through at work, you wouldn't have anything positive to say, either!"* But I know I would not contribute to the problem by adding my negative words to the situation. If we continue to speak and think things that promote negativity, it shouldn't be difficult to understand why our experience at work is negative all the time.

We can begin to cultivate a grateful attitude by waking up each morning, and thanking God for another day and the opportunity to bring income into our households. God loves it when we work with enthusiasm unto Him.

---

*God loves it when we work with
enthusiasm unto Him.*

---

## Write It Down

Habakkuk 2:3 says to write the vision and make it plain so that whoever reads it can run with it. Writing our ideas is a great way to remain focused as we develop a solid work ethic. When we have our thoughts and directives in writing, we can refer to them daily and stay focused on what needs to be done.

I've found that it is best to take time out to make a list of ways in which I can be effective. It is wise to set aside free time to ask yourself questions that will help any company or organization tremendously. *How can I be a blessing to my employer and make my boss's job easier? Are there systems I can implement to be more efficient and effective at what I do?* To get started, it would be greatly beneficial to identify time wasters and time savers.

In addition to writing workplace objectives, we should be more proactive about improving the quality of our work in the future. For example, ask your immediate supervisor what you can do to improve the quality of your work. Hearing directly from your superiors leaves no room for guessing. Inquiring about your job performance demonstrates that you take your job seriously and are determined to give 100 percent. And even if the feedback isn't positive, receive it as constructive criticism. Then make the necessary changes or adjustments. It will pay off!

## Start Early and Leave Late

Most of us know people who consistently get to work late, but they are the first ones out the door when their shift is over. These people will always hinder their own progress. Being disrespectful of the employer's time is one of the biggest mistakes people make at work. These people do not understand the importance of arriving to work on time. As an employer, I can tell the difference in productivity when employees decide to come in late and start wrapping up early. Before long, certain tasks are behind schedule.

It bothers me when I see people nonchalantly drift into work five or ten minutes after their shift starts. I understand emergency situations occur from time to time. However, this should not be the norm. Good employees rarely have emergencies, anyway. But when they do, they are sure to call and let their managers know in a timely manner. This shows they value their employer's time and money. Good employees are in demand these days! Employers want to hire people who will work their shifts and, if necessary, stay until the job is done.

*It bothers me when I see people nonchalantly drift into work five or ten minutes after their shift starts.*

## Loafing on the Job

When people loaf on the job, they are basically not doing what they are paid to do. These are the people we see wasting time, talking on the phone, sending text messages, spending time on Facebook, or doing other unproductive things when they should be working. I believe this is a key reason why some people are not promoted and, in some cases, lose their jobs.

We can be more mindful of our time at work by paying attention to those things that are taking up our time. For example, talking to coworkers can take up a considerable amount of time. Don't get involved in lengthy conversations during the workday. Instead, schedule time during the lunch break to socialize with coworkers. Excessive time spent talking on the company phone, surfing the Internet, and talking with coworkers do not reflect good work ethics.

One way you can better utilize your time at work is to set aside time each day to check your e-mails and to make important phone calls. It may be best to check once in the morning, once in the afternoon, and then right before you leave the office. If you need to make important personal phone calls, do so during your breaks. This way, you use your own time, not the company's time.

## Become Indispensable

While diligent, hard work is essential to seeing success in our lives, there are some specifics we need to consider regarding the *way* we work. As an employer, I want to encourage you to strive to be the type of employee that any employer simply cannot afford to lose. When you build the type of work ethics that display godly character, you become indispensable to your employer.

Here are some things you can do to ensure you are valued by your company:

1. Smile!
2. Try new creative things.

3. Find more effective and efficient ways to do your job.

4. Arrive early and stay late.

5. Treat your company as if it were your own.

Companies are looking for creative individuals they can count on to help them achieve their objectives with excellence. Be that kind of employee, and promotion will be right around the corner!

---

*Companies are looking for creative individuals they can count on to help them achieve their objectives with excellence.*

---

# Life Application

Ask the Holy Spirit to reveal to you areas in which you have become lackadaisical concerning your job or business. Allow Him to help you make the necessary changes and adjustments. Write down what He tells you to do, and create an action plan on how you are going to implement the changes He tells you to make.

_____

_____

_____

_____

_____

_____

_____

_____

_____

# 12

## CHOOSING THE RIGHT PLACE TO LIVE

I have told you these things, so that in Me you
may have [perfect] peace *and* confidence.
In the world you have tribulation *and* trials *and*
distress *and* frustration; but be of good cheer
[take courage; be confident, certain, undaunted]!
For I have overcome the world. [I have deprived
it of power to harm you and have conquered
it for you.]

—JOHN 16:33

And I am convinced *and* sure of this very thing,
that He Who began a good work in you will
continue until the day of Jesus Christ
[right up to the time of His return], developing
[that good work] *and* perfecting *and* bringing
it to full completion in you.

—PHILIPPIANS 1:6

God wants us to live in His divine provision. Therefore, we should allow Him to lead and guide us to the place of His blessing—the place where we will live the good life He has prearranged and made available for us (Ephesians 3:10–20). When we are where He wants us to be, we will have peace, regardless of the situation. We will be able to accomplish more, because we will have the favor that comes only from His blessing. That is why it is imperative that we acknowledge Him first before choosing where we will live.

---

*When we are where He wants us to be, we will have peace, regardless of the situation.*

---

While God has His part to play when we are planning to move, we cannot forget that we have a part to play as well. Our part is to trust Him while using godly wisdom in the practical steps. As we proceed to do our part by actually looking for a home, we must avoid the temptation to rush. When we rush and are overly anxious, we cannot hear from God. For example, early in my marriage, Taffi and I were looking to buy our first home. Every weekend we'd go looking for a house. Basically, I was in a hurry to find a house because I was anxious to get out of the apartment we were living in at the time. I saw a house I wanted to buy, and I showed it to Taffi. She said, "Baby, don't you want to look at another one?" Because I was in such a hurry, I replied, "No, this is fine!" She tried to tell me to choose wisely, but I wouldn't listen.

Not only was I not listening to her, but I wasn't listening to the Holy Spirit, either. Taffi was operating as His helper, and mine, by trying to convince me to slow down and think about the major decision I was about to make. However, I chose to move on with my decision to purchase the house. One night, not long after we moved in, I heard pipes popping! I asked Taffi, "What is that noise?" She said, "That's the house you were in such a hurry to move into and didn't want to thoroughly inspect."

## Our Helper

I've already made it crystal clear how critical it is to our success as Christians to remember to pray and allow the Holy Spirit (Who is our Helper) to direct us in every decision we make. It is equally important to remember to allow peace to be our confirmation. We should allow peace to be our umpire, which requires us spending time alone with the Holy Spirit in prayer.

When we are considering where to live, often everything will seem to line up logically. However, we may not have peace on the inside. Even though things may seem to be perfect on the outside, the Holy Spirit knows *all* things—seen *and* unseen. There may be a situation or challenge awaiting us that we cannot see with the natural eye. Or the timing may be wrong. Because God knows all things, we must trust Him with our lives so we can avoid disaster. Therefore, when there is an absence of peace, we should consult the Holy Spirit for His advice and wisdom, and until we have peace, we must not hesitate to put everything on hold.

*There may be a situation or challenge awaiting us
that we cannot see with the natural eye.*

The other critical part of deciding where to live is deciding which church to attend. God cares, first and foremost, about our spiritual well-being. Some people choose where they want to live first and then decide which church they will attend. However, that is not the proper order. First, we must locate the church God has called us to. We must consider whether or not our service to God will be hindered or enhanced. Here are two important questions we should ask concerning our spiritual growth when planning to relocate:

- Will I be able to focus on my spiritual growth while adjusting to a new job and a new city?

- Is where I plan to move (and the job I choose) going to pull me away from God and the things of God?

Once we pray and bring our consideration before the Lord, the next thing we should do is wait to hear from Him. We should wait for clearance from the Holy Spirit before putting our plan into action. This means taking our time and not rushing through the process of hearing from Him. Too often people act out of excitement, hastiness, and the promise of opportunities before hearing from God. And many times, because of their own desires, some people convince themselves that they have heard from God and proceed to relocate. Unfortunately, in most cases, they learn the hard way that they missed God.

God has an appointed time for you to be in a certain place, and if you rush, you run the risk of missing His best for your life and putting yourself on a detour. In order to avoid wasting your time, money, and energy, trust Him to lead you into the place of His blessing. Seek Him and wait for His answer.

---

*Seek Him and wait for His answer.*

---

## Placement Is Everything

Consider the first place of blessing—the Garden of Eden—where God made man. Adam and Eve were blessed and empowered because they were in the place God had ordained them to be. They had plenty to eat, and they didn't even have to work the ground to reap a harvest. What a life! They could relax and fellowship with their Heavenly Father, and all their needs were taken care of. However, sin changed all of that. As a result of sin, their world completely changed because they were no longer in the place of empowerment. Things that never existed in the Garden of Eden before became a reality in their lives. They had to work hard and till the land in order to eat. Childbearing became a painful experience, and they would have to deal with constant harassment from the devil.

In Genesis 13, Abraham's nephew Lot left his place of empowerment and later experienced tragedy because of where he chose to live. As long as Lot abided with Abraham, he was as blessed as Abraham was. However, because their herdsmen began to strive against one another, the two men decided to part ways. Unfortunately, the place Lot chose to live was not a place of blessing but a place of wickedness that was doomed to destruction:

> *And Lot lifted up his eyes, and beheld all the plain of Jordan, that it was well watered every where, before the Lord*

*destroyed Sodom and Gomorrah, even as the garden of the Lord, like the land of Egypt, as thou comest unto Zoar. Then Lot chose him all the plain of Jordan; and Lot journeyed east: and they separated themselves the one from the other.*

(GENESIS 13:10–11 KJV)

When Lot surveyed the land, all he considered was how fertile it was and how it appeared to flourish. He believed it would be the perfect place for him to relocate and settle with his family. Everything he thought he needed to succeed in life would be at his disposal. His decision was based on what looked good to his eyes and appealed to his senses. It *looked* like a prosperous region, and it seemed to be a good business decision, considering his livelihood.

But it proved to be a poor moral decision that cost Lot his wife and almost cost him his own life. The region was located right outside of Sodom and Gomorrah, which were cities full of immorality and perversion. Ultimately, he and his family ended up having to be rescued, and his wife died in the process of trying to escape God's judgment on the city.

How could something like this happen to a man who thought he was making the right decision? It happened because Lot rationalized his decision and forgot the main ingredient—acknowledging God and allowing Him to lead and guide him to *His* place of blessing.

## A Place Called "There"

God may tell us to go to a particular place, or His instructions may be for us to stay where we are. In either case, we must obey

God. When we don't, we forfeit the blessing He has made available to us. When we do obey Him, we walk in the blessing, and God's provision is seen. For instance, the prophet Elijah was led by God to a specific place where God sustained him. First Kings 17:2–4 says: *"And the word of the Lord came unto him, saying, Get thee hence, and turn thee eastward... and I have commanded the ravens to feed thee there"* (KJV).

---

*When we do obey Him, we walk in the blessing, and God's provision is seen.*

---

The first thing we see in verse 2 is that the Word of the Lord came to Elijah concerning where he was supposed to be. Elijah received instructions from God and was expected to obey. The Lord told Him to go to a *certain* brook because ravens had been provided by God to feed him there. When Elijah arrived at that certain brook, his needs were met.

After Elijah had been sustained by the ravens, verse 7 says, *"And it came to pass after a while, that the brook dried up, because there had been no rain in the land"* (KJV). When this happened, Elijah went back to square one and began seeking God for guidance. He knew he needed another set of instructions from God to get where he was supposed to be next. Like Elijah, we will always need a Word from the Lord in order to get to the place we are supposed to be—that place called "There."

## Dealing with Hurt in the Place called "There"

We should keep in mind that even when the Holy Spirit leads us to that place of blessing and provision, the enemy will try to create situations that will bring feelings of hurt and offense. An example of this is when Believers attend a church where they are getting their spiritual needs met, but when something happens that upsets or offends them, they leave the church. We cannot allow hurt or offense to move us from where God wants us to be. The truth is, God never promised us a life without troubles. Jesus said that in this world we will have tribulation (John 16:33). However, our faith in God's love for us and His grace ensures our victory, even in the midst of trouble. We must trust that His power, which is working within us, has already made us successful (Philippians 1:6).

---

*The enemy will try to create situations that will bring feelings of hurt and offense.*

---

The Bible records the story of Joseph and how he experienced many hardships while he was in the place God called him to be. For instance, Joseph was sold into slavery by his own brothers, and he was thrown into prison for a crime he didn't commit! Through it all, Joseph remembered the covenant God had with him, and he trusted the Lord. All of these situations perfected his character and prepared him to fulfill the will of God for his life. Ultimately, it was in the same place where he suffered many hardships that he was later promoted to vizier and put in charge of all Egypt.

He had endured the hurt, pain, and betrayal. As a result, he had positioned himself to receive influence that he would later use to save his whole family from starvation during a time of famine. What would have happened if Joseph had left the place he had been ordained to be because times were tough for him?

The enemy will use anything he can to distract us and move us out of God's will for our lives. Hurt and offense are his primary tactics. While hurt is inevitable, so is healing. William Shake-speare said, "How poor are they that have not patience! What wound did ever heal but by degrees?" We must trust God to heal our wounds or any hurt we encounter on our way to and in the midst of our place of blessing.

Many times, when we arrive at the place God has called us to, we think we've missed it if we don't see blessings immediately. That is when we really have to press toward what God has for us by remaining focused, diligent, and confident in God's Word, no matter what. Although the road may be bumpy along the way, we will see the rewards if we refuse to quit on God. When we are in the place God has destined us to be, we can trust Him to empower us to do His will. Knowing that we are in the right place will boost our confidence in Him, regardless of what challenges we may face.

---

*Many times, when we arrive at the place God has called us to, we think we've missed it if we don't see blessings immediately.*

---

## Trust in That Place Called "There"

Another person who followed the leading of the Holy Spirit to fulfill the will of God for his life was Abraham. His thinking was limited, and God knew Abraham wasn't going to be able to ful-fill His will for his life by remaining in the land where his rela-tives were. So God began to speak to Abraham so He could lead him to a place where He could bless him and begin a relationship with him. God wanted Abraham to be able to trust Him, but it could not happen as long as his thinking was being shaped by his family and culture. Although Abraham didn't know God (as a matter of fact, he was a moon worshiper), God made a covenant with him to demonstrate how serious He was about His promise to Abraham.

> *Now the Lord had said unto Abram, Get thee out of thy country, and from thy kindred, and from thy father's house, unto a land that I will shew thee: And I will make of thee a great nation, and I will bless thee, and make thy name great; and thou shalt be a blessing: And I will bless them that bless thee, and curse him that curseth thee: and in thee shall all families of the earth be blessed. So Abram departed, as the Lord had spoken unto him.*

> (GENESIS 12:1–4 KJV)

When God's words were backed up by a sworn oath (covenant), Abraham moved away from what was familiar to him and began a new life in another place. Trusting God comes when we develop a personal relationship with Him and allow His Word to govern our lives. Then, when we seek Him for direction, we can be confident that He will lead us exactly where we need to be in order to flourish *and* draw others to Him through the blessing on our lives.

## "There" for Someone Else

Everyone wants to be in the right place so he or she can be blessed and have every need met; however, God's agenda for the blessing is never limited to one person. The ability God put on man to prosper was not just for him but also for the benefit of future generations. As a result of Abraham's obedience, you and I are able to partake of this blessing today! Whenever God gives us something, whether it is a gift, an ability, or a talent, He requires us to use what we have to bless others in some capacity.

For example, if you have been privileged to attend a church where you are fed spiritually, God wants you to share that revelation with someone else. We truly demonstrate we have been blessed when we empower someone else to succeed in life. The same is true when we are blessed in the areas of education, knowledge, expertise, skills, and resources. What we possess can all be used to help someone else become better. When we become a blessing to someone else, that goodness—like a boomerang—will come back to us even greater than the amount we gave.

---

*When we become a blessing to someone else, that goodness—like a boomerang—will come back to us even greater than the amount we gave.*

---

## Practical Things to Consider

Once you find out where God wants you to be, here are some practical tips to consider as you choose a specific area and home. While applying these practical steps, continue to communicate with the Holy Spirit. And definitely allow peace to rule in your heart as you make a decision to move forward with your plans.

1. **Visit the city.** This is so important. There's nothing more critical when deciding where to live than knowing how you feel there; and you can't know that unless you spend some time there. This is a very practical step; however, it also has some spiritual weight.

The Bible tells us to let our peace rule as an umpire (Colossians 3:15). So if you don't have peace when you visit a certain place, then more than likely it is not the place God intends for you to be. Once you visit, if you have peace and feel God is leading you to move, your next step is to talk to people who are familiar with the city. Mention the place you are considering to others and listen to what they have to say about it. Find out about the culture and atmosphere of the area. More than likely, when you talk to people, they will be able to give you valuable information about things you may not have considered.

2. **Don't forget to budget properly.** What would it take to maintain a comfortable lifestyle in that locale? Calculate expenses, such as the price of gas, the transportation system, real estate prices, and the school system. Plan for any unforeseen circumstances, and if you do not already have a job lined up, consider the time it will take you to find one. The last thing you want to do is spend your days stressing out about how you are going to pay your bills.

3. **Choose your surroundings wisely.** Comfort is important when considering a new residence. It is not wise to move in an area where you will feel culturally and socially uncomfortable. For example, if you grew up in a small town where everyone knew you by name and you enjoyed the fact that you always knew what was going on, you probably won't be happy moving into a community where you are just another face in the crowd. If having the small town or slow-paced city experience is important to you, most likely you won't be as comfortable in a big, fast-paced city like Los Angeles or New York. The constant hustle and bustle of living in a metropolitan city such as these may wear you down over time. Consider how you will feel in the long run, once the

initial excitement of the new experience wears off. Again, be sure you are comfortable with your choice and allow it to be a reflection of the things you value. People from different regions of the country (North, South, East, and West) have different ways of thinking and interacting. Cultural and social attitudes differ from region to region. Be sure to examine these aspects, as they may take some time to get used to.

*It is not wise to move in an area where you will feel culturally and socially uncomfortable.*

4. **Don't rush.** Relocating is not a decision you should make overnight. Making decisions in a rush can lead you to a place you don't want to be. Taking your time is practical *and* spiritual, because it allows you to get as much information as possible, and you have time to pray and hear from God. You will be more confident, knowing without a shadow of a doubt that it is God's will. Therefore, do your research. Go online, and read books and magazines, to find out as much as possible about the city you are considering.

*Do your research.*

Again, if God tells you to go to a specific place, you will have to go. But if you have some flexibility, consider choosing a place in which you will feel the most comfortable.

# Life Application

The question to ask today is, "Am I where I am supposed to be?" Make an honest assessment of your life. Write down the reasons you know God has brought you to the place you are now. If you discover you're not where God wants you to be, don't beat yourself up; simply make the adjustment. Pray and ask God to direct you to the city, state, country, or church that will enable you to grow, serve, and experience the good life He has planned for you. Nobody knows your life or purpose like God. He knows what you are supposed to be doing, and where, when, and how you're supposed to be doing it. Listen to His voice, and He will lead you "There."

_____

_____

_____

_____

_____

_____

_____

_____

# 13 CHOOSING THE RIGHT MATE

Now the Lord God said, It is not good
(sufficient, satisfactory) that the man should be
alone; I will make him a helper (suitable, adapted,
complementary) for him.

—GENESIS 2:18

Do not be unequally yoked with unbelievers
[do not make mismated alliances with them
or come under a different yoke with them,
inconsistent with your faith]. For what
partnership have right living *and* right standing
with God with iniquity *and* lawlessness? Or how
can light have fellowship with darkness?

—2 CORINTHIANS 6:14

Living as becomes you] with complete lowliness
of mind (humility) and meekness (unselfishness,
gentleness, mildness), with patience, bearing with
one another *and* making allowances because you
love one another.

—EPHESIANS 4:2

For so long, the practical aspects of this subject have not been dealt with in the church. Two people assume that because they are both Christians and are attracted to each other, they will automatically make suitable marriage partners. However, there is more to consider. In the process of getting to know someone, there are many questions and conversations that must take place in order to gain more knowledge and understanding about a person. In other words, getting to know someone is a vital part of making a wise decision where a mate is concerned.

## A Choice That Makes a Big Difference

The spouse we choose greatly impacts many areas of our lives. One area that is greatly impacted is God's will for our lives. Our marriage partner will affect our calling. Although everyone is not called to pastor, God has a specific assignment for each of us. That's why it is so important that we choose someone who fits into God's plan for our lives. When considering and discovering God's will for our lives, we must be sure to choose a spouse who will complement our calling. It is important to discuss this with our potential mate early in the relationship, and definitely before entering marriage.

Whom you choose to marry will also affect your family. For example, when you and your spouse have children, you cannot change the fact that both of you are the parents of those children. Think of how difficult things will be if you marry someone who turns out to have different spiritual priorities and values than you do. Consider the impact that these disagreements will have on how you raise your children, and how it will affect your ability to minister to them effectively.

---

*Whom you choose to marry will also affect your family.*

---

Your spouse will also affect the quality of life you will have. Think about it. If you choose to marry someone who doesn't believe in financial prosperity or someone who has a poverty mentality, he or she is going to make decisions based on that type of thinking. Therefore, marrying someone who disagrees with you concerning financial prosperity can keep you limited where finances are concerned.

## Seek Wholeness First

Single people should use their time alone to grow in the love of God and allow Him to teach them how to love themselves and others in a godly manner. There may be critical areas in a single person's life that need to be developed or restored before getting married. This will avoid having extra baggage in the marriage as a result of unresolved issues. For instance, if you are a compulsive spender, you may want to resolve that issue before getting married. Your overspending could be the root of many unnecessary disagreements. Or, if you have an issue with lust—that needs to be resolved before you get married. Of course, people can work through things together; however, God's best involves two people who are as whole as possible before getting married. That is why I encourage single people to allow the Holy Spirit to lead them to wholeness before they consider marriage.

*Single people should use their time alone to grow in the love of God and allow Him to teach them how to love themselves and others in a godly manner.*

Wholeness is having peace with who you are. There's nothing missing or broken in your life. Therefore, you are not trying to fill a void that only God can fill. Instead, you are settled in your relationship with Him and have accepted His love for you. You know He is your source, not people or things, and you depend on Him only. In other words, Jesus fulfills everything you need, so there is no need to place unbearable pressure on someone else to fulfill your needs. In fact, it is unfair to try to make someone fill a void that only God can fill.

Many people desire to get married because they believe their identity is confirmed by a mate; but that is not true. God made men and women to complement each other, not define each other. Be sure your identity is established by God *before* entering into a serious relationship. Allow *Him* to define who you are. If you don't allow your identity to be defined by God, you will become desperate to find a mate, ultimately dismiss the Word, and forfeit the successful relationship God desires for you. Establish your identity by studying the Word of God and finding out what He has to say about you.

Psalm 25:14 speaks of the "sweet, satisfying companionship of the Lord." I am a firm believer in the importance of having a strong personal relationship with Jesus Christ before getting married. This is accomplished by communing with Him in prayer and studying His Word on a daily basis. This is a critical aspect of marriage preparation. Again, I want to stress to single people that even on your spouse's best day, he or she will never be able to fulfill you like Jesus can. When we replace Jesus with another person, we will always walk away feeling disappointed.

God's Word offers a wealth of knowledge where relationships and marriage are concerned. In every relationship, we should always make the Word of God our foundation. In order to establish healthy relationships, it is imperative that we allow the teachings of the Bible to be our standard and never compromise. God gives us clear guidelines that if followed will help us build successful relationships and healthy marriages.

*God's Word offers a wealth of knowledge where relationships and marriage are concerned.*

## Seek God, Not a Mate

Developing healthy friendships with those of the opposite sex can become difficult if you are constantly thinking of them as potential mates instead of as friends. In other words, single people shouldn't become so desperate for marriage that they are willing to dismiss the process of establishing healthy relationships. When single people make seeking God their top priority, He will assist them in discovering the right relationships. Matthew 6:33

says, "But seek first his kingdom and his righteousness, and all these things will be given to you as well" (NIV).

When I was single and ready to get married, I simply prayed and asked God for what I wanted in a wife. I knew that I needed a woman of God who had character. I also prayed about my personal physical preferences (though that was not the primary focus). I was very specific in my prayers and released my faith where those things were concerned. After that, I didn't get busy looking for her. I simply made sure that I was in the will of God, doing what He called me to do.

While I was in college, I taught Bible study on the college's campus. One night at Bible study I was praying, and God told me to look up. That was when I saw Taffi! The Lord told me she was what I had been praying for, and He was right! She was exactly what I needed and desired. However, this all happened after I had found the will of God for my life. I was not looking for a hookup. The connection was made because Taffi and I were busy seeking God and His will for our lives. We were in the right place at the right time, doing what God told us to do, and He brought us together. God caused our paths to cross, and we are still happily married today!

When we seek God, He knows how to connect us to the right people. My advice to single people is to stay in faith, no matter how things look or what statistics show, and fight the temptation to get desperate. Instead, devote yourself to God. When you begin to love and serve the Lord with all of your might, you will enjoy your current season of singleness while expecting God to do a marvelous thing in your life. He will give you the desires of your heart!

*When we seek God, He knows how to*
*connect us to the right people.*

## Unequally Yoked

Primarily, one of the first things you want to know before choosing a mate is whether or not he or she is a Christian. Second Corinthians 6:14 says Believers should not be unequally yoked with unbelievers. Unfortunately, I have counseled numerous single Christians who were convinced that God told them to marry someone who was not a Christian. This type of thinking opposes the Scriptures, and God never opposes His Word. If you are a Christian, God requires you to marry another Christian— no exceptions. Therefore, while you are dating, make sure your special someone is living according to the Word of God. This will protect you from a lot of confusion, chaos, and disappointment down the road.

In a marriage, both parties have a part to play and an exchange to make, which is to edify each another. A Christian is not going to be edified by a spouse who practices a different religion. You won't be able to connect spiritually because Jesus is not at the center of your beliefs. If your belief systems do not align, there will be conflict in your relationship.

*A Christian is not going to be edified by a spouse who practices a different religion.*

It is also important that you marry a Christian who is on the same spiritual level as you are regarding growth, maturity, and understanding of God's Word. For example, if you have been saved many years and have experienced deeper revelations of God's Word, it probably wouldn't be the best idea to marry someone who just became born again. Your spouse may not understand the revelations you receive from God's Word, which can lead to frustration, especially once the honeymoon is over. When your individual beliefs and values concerning the Word of God begin to clash, it won't be long before it becomes a source of tension and frustration in your marriage. This is particularly true with many women who marry unsaved men, or have husbands who aren't on fire for the Lord. Trying to drag your husband to church every Sunday when he would rather sleep in can drive a wedge between you.

## Respect Your Parents' Judgment

Another important component of selecting a spouse is respecting your parents' judgment. No matter how old you are, be open to listening to your parents' observations about the individual you want to marry. They know you better than most people. They also are more likely to have your best interests at heart. Of course there are situations where parents' opinions and motives for advising their son or daughter are wrong. However, allow your parents to speak openly and honestly about their feelings and instincts concerning a potential mate and be willing to listen and even end the relationship if necessary. Most of the time, they will be right, whether their response is positive or negative.

Ephesians 6:1 says, *"Children, do what your parents tell you. This is only right. Honor your father and mother"* (MSG). When you honor your parents, you honestly consider their opinion; you take into account what they say and act on it.

The great thing about allowing your parents to give you their thoughts is that they will often see something you have missed. They will ask questions you may have never thought of asking. The truth is, sometimes when you meet a person and you think he or she is the greatest thing since sliced bread, you overlook critical areas that may cause problems later. This is why it is so important to allow other people to meet him or her. If you don't have parents who are able to offer advice, find a godly married couple who can guide you and give you insight into the person's character.

When you refuse counsel regarding your new relationship, it is because you probably know something is not right, and you just don't want to be told. But when the Word of God is your final authority, you will seek godly counsel as the Word instructs us to. Proverbs 15:22 says, *"Refuse good advice and watch your plans fail; take good counsel and watch them succeed"* (MSG). If you are truly interested in establishing a healthy relationship that will last, seek godly counsel.

## Collect Data

The dating phase is the time to collect data. It provides the couple with many opportunities to engage in lengthy conversation. Divorce and hurt feelings can be avoided when you ask wise questions and get the necessary information at the beginning of the relationship. Regardless of what today's society depicts, marriage is designed to be a permanent institution that lasts forever. That's why it is wise to be informed before making such a life-changing decision. When we take the time to obtain a substantial amount of detailed information, we are more equipped to make a quality decision.

*When we take the time to obtain a substantial amount of detailed information, we are more equipped to make a quality decision.*

A good marriage can be like days of Heaven on Earth, but a bad marriage can be likened to days of Hell on Earth. Unfortunately, many couples I have counseled over the years have not found this out until after saying "I do"—mainly because they failed to ask the right questions, heed godly counsel, and take enough time to get to know their potential spouses. Finding out God's will for marriage, relationships, and the process of getting to know someone can save you a lot of time and problems.

It is God's will to give you a husband or wife if you truly desire to be married. Arming yourself with information and knowing what questions to ask will position you to receive from Him. When God does bring someone into your life, you will be prepared and knowledgeable about how to choose a mate according to the guidelines He has given you in His Word, and your marriage will be based on a solid foundation.

However, while you are single, it is important to be thankful for where you are at this time. Enjoy your single life and use it as an opportunity to get closer to God and discover His will for your life. Begin to enjoy your uniqueness and everything special about you. Allow Him to help you heal from past hurts and disappointments. More important, allow His love for you to lead you to wholeness.

# Life Application

The dating process is the time when you really get to know each other. It should be a purposeful time, designated to ask certain practical questions in order to determine if you and your potential spouse are truly compatible. Below are key questions to ask during this process. As you ask yourself these questions concerning the compatibility of your potential spouse, be sure to pray and ask the Holy Spirit for guidance when answering these questions.

If you are married, these questions can still be considered and worked through to enhance your relationship. If you discover there are some questions you've never answered, make a decision to resolve them so your marriage can go to the next level.

Record the answer to these questions in the space provided when considering a potential spouse:

1. Is he/she of the Christian faith?

2. What kind of Christian is he/she?

3. Is this person truly committed to loving and obeying God?

4. Are we compatible where spiritual things are concerned?

5. Do we agree on the major doctrines of the Bible (salvation, healing, deliverance, speaking in tongues, etc.)?

6. Do we agree on the church we will attend?

7. Do we agree on where we will spend our time and money?

8. Can I trust this person?

9. Has this person given me any reason not to trust anything he/she has said or done?

10. How does he/she handle adversity?

11. Does this person believe in God, or does he/she fall into unbelief regularly?

12. Have I ever seen this person angry?

13. Has he/she been angry with me?

14. Are we able to resolve conflict in a biblical way?

15. Was forgiveness granted or was the issue just swept under the rug?

16. Does he have the means to provide for me?/Do I have the means to provide for her?

17. Is he/she responsible with money?

18. Is he/she a good example of Christianity?

19. What issues do we agree or disagree on?

20. Does this person have control over his/her sex drive?

21. Do I feel pressured to have sex?

22. Does he/she respect me?

23. Does he/she listen to me and consult me before making decisions?

24. Is this person truly open to my input?

25. Is there mutual submission?

26. Have we resolved conflicts lovingly?

27. How does he/she treat other people?

28. Have I dated this person long enough to have an idea of what he/she struggles with every day?

29. Can I live with the areas in which he/she is not doing very well?

30. Is this a giving person, or is he/she selfish?

31. Do we communicate effectively?

32. Is he/she my best friend?

33. Is he/she divorced? If so, is there an understanding about why he/she is divorced?

# CONCLUSION

He has made everything beautiful in its time.
He also has planted eternity in men's hearts *and*
minds [a divinely implanted sense of a purpose
working through the ages which nothing under
the sun but God alone can satisfy]...

—ECCLESIASTES 3:11A

Such hope never disappoints *or* deludes *or* shames
us, for God's love has been poured out in our
hearts through the Holy Spirit Who has been
given to us.

—ROMANS 5:5

Throughout this book, I've shared with you the various ways in which the Holy Spirit guides us into God's ultimate plan for our lives. I have shown you that through His role as Counselor, the Holy Spirit is also a financial advisor. That means we don't have to worry about issues concerning our finances. He will help us to gain all the resources we need to accomplish the will of God for our lives.

Unfortunately, there are many Christians who believe they are destined to a life without any direction or success. There are also Christians who believe they are doomed to a poverty-stricken life in which there is no hope. However, anyone who has studied the Bible can clearly see a continued theme woven throughout the Scriptures—God loves us and He wants to bless us abundantly. His plan for our lives exceeds anything we could ever hope or dream (Ephesians 3:20). By His Spirit, He strengthens us where we are weak, imparts wisdom when we're confused, and directs us when we're lost.

---

*God loves us and He wants to bless us abundantly.*

---

Jesus said that the Holy Spirit would be in close fellowship with us throughout our lives. He stated in John 16:7, *"However, I am telling you nothing but the truth when I say it is profitable (good, expedient, advantageous) for you that I go away. Because if I do not go away, the Comforter (Counselor, Helper, Advocate, Intercessor, Strengthener, Standby) will not come to you [into close fellowship with you]; but if I go away, I will send Him to you [to be in close fellowship with you]."* The Holy Spirit has been sent as a precious promise to Christians.

Here is a summary of the functions, attributes, and characteristics of the Holy Spirit:

- The Holy Spirit is not an emotion or any other outward manifestation such as "falling out." However, His presence affects our emotions because humans are emotional beings.

- The Holy Trinity is God the Father, God the Son, and God the Holy Spirit: the three make up one Godhead (1 John 5:6–7).

- He is the motivator, energizer, and operator of every revealed plan or vision from God. He is in charge of the affairs of the kingdom of God and is the chief executor of divine programs on earth (Acts 1:8; Acts 2:1–21; Acts 10:39–47; Acts 11:15–17; Acts 19:1–7, 21; Romans 8:26–30 NLT).

- He is the revealer of the hidden treasures of the kingdom of God (1 Corinthians 14:2 NLT).

- He holds the key to the inheritance of the saints of God.

- He is the most valuable asset in Christian living.

- He is the central figure in any breakthrough in life.

- He is the Spirit of Truth and has been sent to reveal the mind of God to those who are born again (John 16:12–15 NLT).

- He wants to reveal your God-nature to you and cause you to live on a level higher than the one you are living on right now.

- He is a real person with whom you must develop a real relationship.

- He is your invisible partner, giving you inside information.

- He is the oil of joy (Isaiah 61:3). You cannot be filled with the Holy Spirit and not have joy in your life, because He literally injects the Believer with joy and gladness.

- He pours the love of God in the hearts of those who make Jesus Christ their Lord and Savior (Romans 5:5).

The foundation of God's kingdom is love. We need to believe in God's love in order to operate successfully in the kingdom of God. In Ephesians, Paul prayed a special prayer. He prayed that the Believers in Ephesus would know and experience the love of God like never before:

*For this reason [seeing the greatness of this plan by which you are built together in Christ], I bow my knees before the Father of our Lord Jesus Christ, for Whom every family in heaven and on earth is named [that Father from Whom all father-hood takes its title and derives its name]. May He grant you out of the rich treasury of His glory to be strengthened and reinforced with mighty power in the inner man by the [Holy]*

*Spirit [Himself indwelling your innermost being and personality]. May Christ through your faith [actually] dwell (settle down, abide, make His permanent home) in your hearts! May you be rooted deep in love and founded securely on love.*

EPHESIANS 3:14–17

Paul made it clear that there is a connection between God's might and His love! As Believers, we *must* be rooted and grounded in His love in order to live successfully. The more we realize God's love for us, the more we become strengthened as individuals. When we believe that He loves us, our faith works, and we are strengthened by His power as it works inside us. His power helps us function effectively as Christians on a day-to-day basis.

---

*The more we realize God's love for us, the more we become strengthened as individuals.*

---

In your life, begin to examine the many ways God has expressed His love for you through the leadership of the Holy Spirit. Are you giving Him the credit for the victories in your life? Whether He has guided you to the right church, the right mate, the right place to live, or the right career, don't forget to give Him all the glory and praise! Remember, the Holy Spirit is not an *it* but an actual person. He's your unseen partner. Therefore, continue to lean on, rely on, and trust in Him. And with every success you have, every obstacle you overcome, and every victory you win, know without a shadow of a doubt that the Holy Spirit is not just your financial advisor. He is an expression of God's unfailing love for you.

# NOTES

1. Andrew Wommack, "Spirit, Soul, and Body," Andrew Wommack Ministries, http://www.awmi.net/extra/article/spirit_soul.

2. ("Top Trends of 2011: Maximizing Spiritual Change," Barna Group, http://www.barna.org/faith-spirituality/547-top-trends-of-2011-maximizing-spiritual-change).